Interface Design & Document Design

Interface Design & Document Design

Editors:
Piet Westendorp
Carel Jansen
Rob Punselie

Amsterdam - Atlanta, GA 2000

ISBN 90 - 420 - 0510 - 6

Colophon
Edited by: P.H. Westendorp, C.J.M. Jansen, R. Punselie
Design: Plaza ontwerpers b.v., www.poe.nl
Printed in the Netherlands

The paper on wich this book is printed meets the
requirements of "ISO 9706: 1994, information and
documentation - Paper for documents -
Requirements for permanence"

Publisher
Rodopi
Tijnmuiden 7
1046 AK Amsterdam
The Netherlands
www.rodopi.nl

Preface

Interaction with complex devices can progress via two different routes: via the user interface or via the supporting documentation. These two routes are usually created by design groups with totally different backgrounds and interests. As a result, the user interface and the documentation often do not match. This book focuses on the relationship that should exist between the two disciplines within which user interfaces and documents are created. Researchers from several universities and interface designers and documentation designers from the world's leading companies share their views on the development and further integration of user interface design and document design. The book is organized along two lines. First the integration and development of online help, wizards, guides and documentation is treated, then the implications for a specific target group (the elderly) are discussed.

This book is the written product of the Interface Design & Document Design conference, held at Eindhoven University of Technology on May 28 and 29, 1998. The conference was organized by Eindhoven University of Technology, the Institute for Perception Research (IPO) and the Netherlands Society for Technical Information and Communication (STIC). The organizing committee consisted of members from each of these organizations: Floor van Horen, Aad Houtsma, Carel Jansen, Rob Punselie, Rini Weijman and Piet Westendorp. The contributions to this book - a selection from presentations and workshops - have been corrected by Paul Bakker from Peterborough Technical Communications - we owe him many thanks for the painfully accurate streamlining of all the texts. Our last thank you is for Ellen Altenburg for her patient efforts at editing the final lay-out.

In this book, there are many illustrations and references to email-addresses and websites. All illustrations in this book and some additional illustrations to the texts, plus summaries of all the texts can be viewed in full-color on the STIC website www.stic.nl. Any updates of email-addresses and websites mentioned in this book will also be listed.

Eindhoven, March 2000
Piet Westendorp
Carel Jansen
Rob Punselie

Contents

Parallels and dichotomies in Interface Design & Document Design

Piet Westendorp[@]
Carel Jansen[@]
Rob Punselie[@]

If you can't explain it, don't design it.

Summary

The design of the user interface and the design of supporting documents often do not match; they may differ strongly in both content and presentation. This is caused by the separate design and production processes of user interfaces and additional help in most organizations. Because of the increasing complexity of technological products, there seems to be a growing consciousness that the user interface and the supporting instructional documentation should be considered and designed in close cooperation. Designers should realize that users may build two different types of mental models when trying to operate a device, using both the user interface and the documentation. Further integration of the design of user interfaces and user instructions may lead to a more effective and efficient use of modern technological products. If designers work together more closely, this may reduce the risk that users construct conflicting mental models of one and the same product.

1 Forms dichotomy

About a decade ago, Sony developed the *My First Sony* line of products. These were simple radios, alarms, cassette-players and other electronic consumer products. The designs expressed clearly that these products were made for children: all plastic, bright primary colors (very much like the colors of Lego bricks), rounded corners, big buttons, sturdily built, clear product graphics, and so on. This line of products was an immediate sales success[1] and the design was quickly copied by several competitors. One of these 'me-too-products' from a competitor is the *Video Painter* graphic tablet. For this product, in much the same way,

---

[@]   p.h.westendorp@io.tudelft.nl
[@]   c.jansen@let.kun.nl
[@]   rob@punselie.com
[1]   Children liked them, but it is noteworthy that also elderly people appeared to buy these products because of their nice big buttons, big displays and clear products graphics.

every detail expresses that this is a toy, not a tool.

The Video Painter graphic tablet can be connected to a TV and it is comparable to *Paint* software. It has quite a few functions (including some games) and - as a result - it is not so easy to use. Informal tests confirmed this hypothesis. To make optimal use of this product, most users will have to consult the manual. This is not to blame the designers of the product, it is standard for all products that have many features. But while the design of the user interface of this product so clearly suggests that it is a toy for children, the design of the user manual just as clearly suggests that it was designed for an elderly civil servant. It is a black and white document with a boring lay-out, only very few pictures, an ugly typeface and a very low print quality (probably from a low dpi dot matrix printer). Moreover, it gives the distinct impression that the text was written by a retired technician with strong interest in formal contract writing from the end of the last century. The illustrations must have been produced by a technical illustrator specializing in electronic circuit diagrams. It is an understatement that the Interface Design & the Document Design of the Video Painter do not match. Immediately after unpacking, the joy of the product is destroyed by the sadness of the manual.

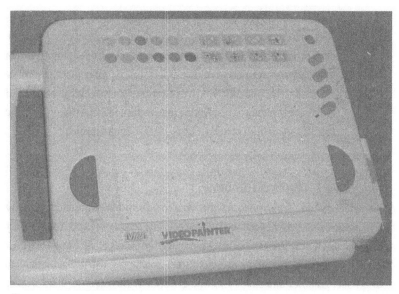

Figure 1.
The Video Painter graphic tablet: a toy designed for children.

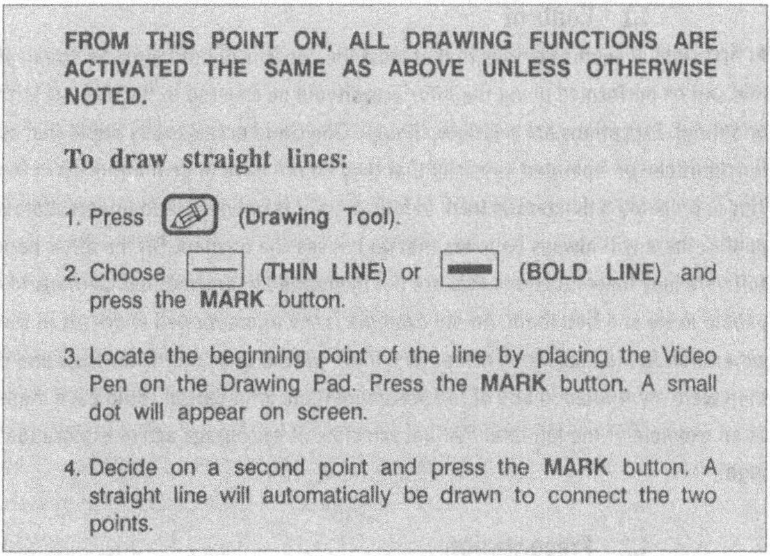

FROM THIS POINT ON, ALL DRAWING FUNCTIONS ARE
ACTIVATED THE SAME AS ABOVE UNLESS OTHERWISE
NOTED.

To draw straight lines:

1. Press ⬛ (Drawing Tool).

2. Choose ⬛ (THIN LINE) or ⬛ (BOLD LINE) and
   press the MARK button.

3. Locate the beginning point of the line by placing the Video
   Pen on the Drawing Pad. Press the MARK button. A small
   dot will appear on screen.

4. Decide on a second point and press the MARK button. A
   straight line will automatically be drawn to connect the two
   points.

Figure 2.
The Video Painter graphic tablet manual: a tool designed for technical professionals.

This contrast between the style of the product user interface and the style of the document interface of the Video Painter graphic tablet may be an extreme example of a mismatch between product user interface design and document design, but it is rather more the rule than the exception that the design of user interfaces of devices, and the design of documents do not match. Style is only one aspect of possible differences between the designs of each of these two kinds of products. The *design of a device interface* may refer to various aspects, such as functionality and structuring of the functions, grouping, lay-out and design of buttons, handles and display, use of color and product graphics. The *design of an information interface* also refers to various aspects, such as content and structuring of the information and overall concept of the document, lay-out of the individual pages, syntax and wording, design of the graphic elements, use of color and the typography. *Design* may involve both *content* and *presentation* and presentation may concern both *style* and *ergonomics* of the product user interface and documentation. Of course, one could argue that we are comparing incomparable products: the interface of a technical device, for instance an electronic appliance or software, and the interface of the information, usually resulting in a (printed) manual. But it is obvious that there must be a close relation in the design (as defined above) between the two. If the product interface gives the user a somewhat different idea of what the product can do and how to do that from what the documentation does, there is a mismatch between the *design* of the device interface and the *design* of the document. The differences may concern both *content* and *presentation*.

1.1   Content

At first sight, it seems obvious that at least the *content* of both must be equal: all functions that can be performed using the interface, should be covered in the manual (either on paper or online). Exceptions are possible, though. One could occasionally argue that some functions can be operated so easily that they do not have to be mentioned in the manual. This is probably a dangerous track to follow, as 'it is impossible to underestimate a vast public': there will always be users that do not see the obvious. On the other hand, computer software may have functions that are not mentioned in any manual, perhaps to invite people to try and find them. An old example is the unmentioned shortcuts in the first generation Apple Macintosh computers; there proved to be more shortcuts and functions than were mentioned in any of the documentation. John Carroll could have mentioned these as an example of the Minimal Manual principle of 'encourage active exploration' (Carroll, 1990).

1.2   Presentation

Most people will agree that the *style* of the manual should reflect the image of the product. The style is the first aspect of the design that users perceive, both on the product user interface and in the documentation. On a device, the style is defined by the shape of buttons, handles, display and other elements, use of color and product graphics. The visual style of the documentation is defined by lay-out, design of the graphic elements, use of color, typography and other aspects; the textual style is defined by syntax and wording. The example of the Video Painter mentioned above is a clear example of a visual design of a document that does not have the style that the product has[2]. Especially products with a high brand image (which is usually reflected by the style of the user interface) need documentation that is designed with a matching style. Buyers of a Rolls-Royce automobile, a Bang & Olufson television set or a Leica camera would be unpleasantly surprised to receive a number of deteriorated black-and-white copies stapled together when they collect their new car, TV or camera from the dealer.

Perhaps most important, *ergonomic* aspects of the presentation of the device user interface and the presentation of the document interface also have to be in line with each other. Ergonomic aspects of the presentation of a device user interface concern the structuring of functions and navigation tools, grouping and lay-out of buttons, handles and display, (ergonomic) use of color and product graphics. Ergonomic aspects of a document interface presentation concern structuring of the information, navigation and overall concept of the document, lay-out of individual pages, (ergonomic) use of color and textual aspects such as syntax and wording. The need for integration and overlap in presentation of these elements is discussed by several authors contributing to this book.

---

2   In fact, the textual style of the documentation did not match the style of the product either.

Of course, device interfaces and information interfaces differ in many respects. Some examples may show the variety of possible differences.

- A user manual that simply describes the functions of all the menu-items one after the other is generally considered not to be a good manual, exactly because it is not user-oriented, but function-oriented (one might even say 'button-oriented'). Such a manual is easy to write, but unhelpful when the user wants to perform tasks or has a specific problem.
- Photographs may present the most exact representations of the elements, but they are generally considered not to be most efficient for users (for instance, because they show too many details); more abstract black and white line drawings are often far more useful.
- It may be useless to repeat the color-schemes used to indicate which buttons concern the same type of functionality (for instance a green background for the number-buttons on a remote control for a VCR) in the manual. On the other hand, too often this visual support of the user interface is not fully exploited in the manual.
- The use of a product may sometimes best be expressed with a manual that is basically a flowchart (see figure 3). The device interface does not necessarily have to express this flowchart concept (although it might also be an idea for some product interfaces).

The design of a device user interface and the design of documentation cannot match completely if we compare a device with a printed manual. But the designs have to overlap much more when both the user interface of the product and the interface of the information are presented on-line. Clearly, the structuring of the information must have some relationship with the structuring of the buttons or menu-items; color-schemes used in the user interface are preferably reflected in the manual or the online help, and illustrations in the manual should have a good resemblance to the depicted elements of the product interface. Navigation elements that guide users through the Help should reflect the navigation elements that guide the user through the product's functionality. Differences could be useful, though: with the ongoing integration of the Help into the functionality of the software, it might be necessary to make clear what is Help and what is not - there might be good arguments not to integrate Interface Design & Document Design completely.

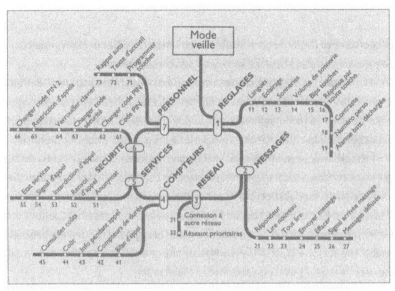

Figure 3.
Bosch manual, showing the functions of a mobile phone. It might be helpful for the product user interface to be based on the same idea as this manual is; every function immediately traceable and selectable, and a one-to-one relationship with the manual.

2   Causes

There are other reasons why product interface design and document design are usually worlds apart. In many companies, product design (which often includes user interface design) and manual production are two completely separated organizational routes; often, they are produced by two different departments. User interfaces are usually developed in close cooperation with the development and marketing of product features and documentation literally and figuratively comes last. The documentation or help is designed when the product is finished. A document designer may discover that some things are almost impossible to explain or instruct, for instance because they are very counter - intuitive, but his or her comments may come too late - and are often unwanted. Production has already started and the manuals have to be ready yesterday. There is no time to think about the design at all, let alone time to listen to the comments of the document designers and reconsider the device interface. These first 'testers of the product' are often experienced in noticing the communicative shortcomings of user interface aspects. Often, it would have been beneficial to the quality of the product, if the observations of the document designers had been taken into account.

An example of a product with an interface that makes good document design a very difficult task, is the Sony RM-816 remote control for television sets. This is a two-sided remote control that can be slid into a hard plastic holder. One side is for day-to-day use; the other side for programming and other more advanced functions[3]. People who want to use one of the advanced functions, press two buttons on the sides of the holder, lift the remote control out of the holder, turn it around and slide it in again until it clicks in. Then they have a wealth of buttons to choose from. But for programming, some buttons (like: 'store') that seem to be necessary are not on the remote control. Yet, the manual mentions them and shows the icons. The user may try the other side of the remote control again, but no, the buttons are not there. The user may try and reverse the remote control again, but will probably not find all of the programming buttons. It takes many users quite a while to find out that some buttons on the programming side appear to be hidden in the holder, when the remote control is slid in (see figure 4). They have to pull it out a little bit to be able to touch some of the buttons that are necessary for programming (see figure 5). A document designer may put this in the manual 'in neon lights', but many users will not notice this, simply because the design of the product showed them the wrong direction, which seemed so obvious and intuitive: for programming, use the programming side-period. A minor change in the design of the holder (e.g. 1 centimeter more open space) would have avoided the whole problem. Now, the document designer gets an impossible task, simply because there was no cooperation between the Interface Designer & the Document Designer.

In many companies that produce high-tech products, the help is considered less important because it is after sales, whereas the user interface is pre-sales, and that is where the money is. This seems a regrettably short-sighted view, possibly triggered by the urge for product managers to meet short-term targets. A product with a smart looking interface and a poor manual (be it because of content or presentation) may sell well anyway. But when the customer cannot get the newly bought microwave-oven, camera or spreadsheet with all these magnificent functions to do what it should do, the brand image that has been created with so much design, marketing and advertising money, may be devalued completely within minutes. Product managers do not always realize what this may do to the marketing of the next generation of their products and to the image of other products that are marketed by the same company. In many major companies, the relation between product's Interface Design and Document Design can be characterized as 'Penny Wise, Pound Foolish'[4].

---

3   A sales assistant once called the side with the programming functions the 'daddy side' and the side with just the day-to-day functions the 'mommy side'. The (female) customer left the shop without buying the TV.

4   Schriver (1979: p. 212-223) found that 79% of the respondents in a customer survey considered the quality of the manual to be an argument to buy a product of the same make next time and that 84% thought that companies should advertise the quality of their manuals.

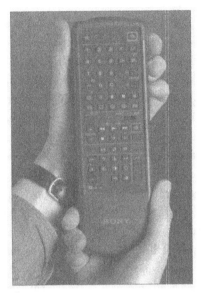

Figure 4.
The Sony RM-816 remote control;
programming side in the holder.

Figure 5.
The Sony RM-816 remote control; programming
side slightly drawn out of the holder.
Now the vital programming buttons at the
bottom are visible.

3   Turning tide

Processors and memory chips have become very powerful and very cheap and that process
is still going on[5]. Electronic products now already have many functions and each new
release will have many more new functions. As a result, these products are already very
complex to use and will be even more difficult to use. This may cause the criterion for a
marketing success to move away from technology to communication. Marketing success may
no longer depend upon the number of functions, but rather on the communication of these
functions. This communication will not just be the pre-sales communication, like the user
interface and the marketing communication (advertising), but also the instructions for use.
Right now, this may still seem wishful thinking on the part of document designers, but
especially in the software sector, there are some indications of a turning tide. The most
obvious reason why companies have learned to listen more to document designers is that
helpdesks have proved to be necessary and expensive and that many complaints and
questions could have been avoided by having a good manual[6]. Saving on the manual means
spending on the helpdesk instead[7].

5   Moore's Law gives an indication of the increasing performance of microchips: Gordon Moore noticed in 1964 that
     up to that time the performance of the microchip had doubled every year. In later years the definition has
     changed (with Gordon Moore's approval) to reflect that doubling occurs every 18 months.
6   http://www.cyberjuice.com/helpdeskfunnies/index.htm
7   See Redish, J. & Ramey, J. (1995), Measuring the value added by professional technical communicators.
     Technical Communication 42, p. 23-86.

This turning of the tide may be expressed by the results of some recent surveys concerning the use and appreciation of manuals. Schriver (1997, pp. 209-223) found that 94% of her subjects use the manual that comes with electronic products. This confirms prior research that indicated that manuals are used widely (Petersen, 1984, Wright, 1981) - in contrast to what seems to be generally believed. Schriver's research also shows an increase in the use of instructions in comparison to this prior research, and this may well be explained by the increasing complexity of the products. We simply cannot use modern (electronic) products without the manual anymore, just as we would not be able to use them without user interfaces (imagine how to operate a VCR if you would have to connect the wires yourself instead of pressing buttons).

4   Integration

The most interesting cause for a turning of the tide may be the development towards further integration of user instructions in product interfaces. In modern software, the Help already is integrated into the program. Buyers will consider the Help as belonging to the interface, comparable to the grouping of menu-items and buttons, design of direct manipulation buttons, use of color-schemes, and so on. This process will continue: the Help will increasingly be considered an essential part of the product interface. It will co-determine the user interface. An intriguing example of this integration is the World Wide Web, which started as - and to a high degree still is - a huge compilation of documents. Interface Design here means, to a large extent Document Design.

The browser (interface design) and pages (document design) could at first easily be separated as different elements. But with the use of other data formats (sound, animation, video), web-pages can hardly be called 'documents' anymore. Nowadays, plug-ins such as Java and Flash provide increasing interactivity to web documents. In fact they provide them with an interface of their own. This means that one cannot only click toward other pages with information, but that one can actually *operate* products from a distance[8]. On the web, document design thus develops into interface design[9]. With new web standards - such as XML - this trend will only increase. Now, more and more, the interface design becomes dominant: not just the design of the navigation and the selection of information on pages, but the design of an interface that controls a product, whether elements on the website itself or other software or indeed hardware (such as a video camera). Moreover, the

---

8   Nice examples concerning the integration of Interface Design & Document Design can be seen and used at http://www.livemanuals.com and at http://207.97.150.242/instructions/animations.html

9   An interesting reverse angle can be found in software agents (or 'intelligent agents'), small pieces of software that assist users by autonomously performing specific tasks on their behalf, such as information retrieval or price negotiations. This could be interpreted as software (including an interface) focusing on document design related issues. http://www.cis.udel.edu/~agents98/ http://pattie.www.media.mit.edu/people/pattie/ For more links to intelligent agents, see the references in José Arcellana's Designing Assistants in this volume.

combination of navigation through information and controlling of remote software or hardware, plus instructions to do so, will make websites much more complex than they are nowadays and make Help more vital.

This development of complete integration of product interface and instructions for use has only just started. Until recently, help was provided online by the program, but users not only had to find the information they needed themselves, they also had to feed this information back into the computer that obviously already knows this information. Probably version 1 of WordPerfect for the Macintosh was the first software with integrated interactive help. Once the user had selected a subject, the program not only offered the procedural information, but also an 'Execute' button in the Help with which users could immediately perform the action (see figure 6). The instructions were presented, such that the user could enter them in the computer manually, but the computer could also perform the task if the user just hit the 'Execute' button. As a result, the user did not have to learn how to perform this task anymore. This means that the online-help in fact provided the user with an alternative user interface for performing the task. Theoretically, in such a situation (if all functions could have been operated in this way), the user could perform all tasks without using the 'standard' user interface (menus, menu-items); he or she could always simply immediately select the Help, find the function and press the 'Execute' button. It may be a bit of an exaggeration because it seems impossible to apply this 'Execute' button for all tasks, but one could suggest to completely replace the product user interface (consisting of menus, menu-items, and so on) with just the Help interface.

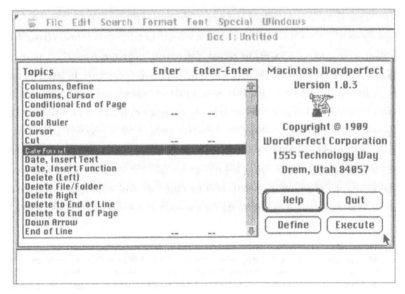

Figure 6.
Help in WordPerfect for the Macintosh version 1.05. Notice the 'Execute' button.

Remarkably, WordPerfect discontinued this functionality in the Help, but Microsoft introduced it in the Office 95 Help and further developed it in Office 97 and Office 2000. In MS Office, the user asking for help not only gets information, but may also get a wizard that guides him or her in performing the task immediately from within the help function. The contribution of Hoek & Kaufman in this book presents an excellent overview of this development and makes clear that Microsoft intends to proceed along this line of integrating Interface Design & Document Design.

5   Mental representations

Users perceive and learn the functions of a product in various ways:
1. by operating the product user interface (icons, buttons, and so on)
2. by consulting the help (printed manual or the basic online help)
3. via all other kinds of instructional information (error messages, wizards, agents, context sensitive help, cue cards, coaches, demos, tutorials, classroom trainings).

By using the interface, by consulting the help and by perceiving all the other information, users develop a kind of mental model (for technical products sometimes termed a *device model*) of that product: a little theory of how this product functions or should be operated. This device model will be adapted or refined during use of the product and may always change.

Moreover (4), users may already have a simple form of a device model even before they have used the product. This elementary device model has been developed on the basis of all kinds of pre-sales information, both commercial and non-commercial. Users may have seen advertising (commercials, brochures) or received other pre-sales information (from the reseller or from the neighbor). The device model will also be developed on the basis of association of the new product with products that they know[10]. A user who buys a new VCR will develop a mental model of this VCR on the basis of the ones he or she already used. In the case of a complete new type of product, the user will develop a mental model on the basis of a comparison with existing products that have similar functionality. For instance, a user who has just bought new hardware and software to record broadcasted programs onto a hard disk, may *a priori* have the idea that such recording will be similar to that with a VCR, because a VCR has a comparable main function: recording and reproducing broadcasted programs. For an overview of the development of the user's device model see figure 7.

---

10   Hackos & Redish (1998, p. 408) present a nice diagrammatic overview of all the communication tools that provide information or instruction for users of technical products. This diagram also shows the proximity of the various tools related to the product and the user. Unfortunately, Hackos & Redish do not include the pre-sales information.

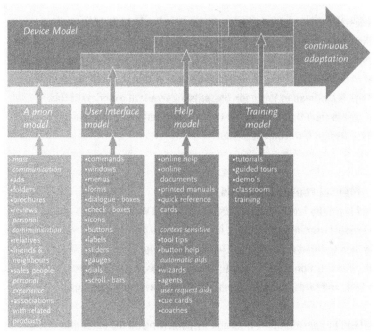

Figure 7.
Development of the user's device model on the basis of various sources of information: a priori information, user interface, help and training aids. This diagram shows the combination of influences on the user's device model, based on both User Interface and Documentation aspects. The various sub-models may interfere or even conflict with each other. Note that some items could be classified as both User Interface and Help elements (e.g. tool tips, button help, wizards, agents, cue cards and coaches).
This diagram also expresses increasing user initiative in searching for information over time - from passively receiving information (a priori) to actively searching for information (training aids).

An interesting question is whether the user of a product that comes with a manual and/or online help, builds up just one device model, based on the user interface with support from the manual, or two different device models (one based on the visual interface and one based on the instructions in the manual) or two different ones, depending on the degree to which additional help was used. The device model that a user builds up or develops by just trying out all buttons might well be different from the device model that a user builds up by consulting the manual or online help. The latter activity implies following a different learning track and, in doing this, the user may perceive the functionality of the product differently, even if he or she has used the same functions of the product (see figures 8 & 9). It is conceivable that the user who learns just by trying out the product user interface (control panel), develops a mental representation of the product that is first of all based on the location and recognition of the elements, whereas the user who consults the manual for (and before) each task, may develop a model based on procedural instructions. The first user might build up a model that consists of an overall idea of lay-out and form; the second might build up a model that basically consists of a series of procedures.

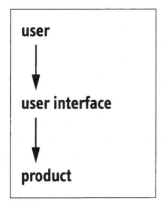

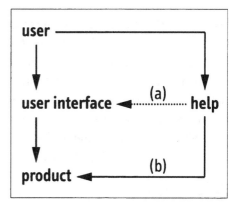

Figure 8.
User learns just by using the product user interface.

Figure 9.
User learns by using product user interface plus help (a) or by purely using the (interactive) help interface (b).

Often, this difference will also be reflected in the opposition of pictorial elements (on-screen buttons, and so on) and textual instructions. One could hypothesize that instructions would be more efficient and effective if they would be, as much as possible, a one-to-one copy of the visual product user interface elements (icons, buttons, and so on). The cognitive load would then be minimal, because users perceive the instruction in exactly the same form as the objects that they have to manipulate. No media transition would be necessary - and there is some evidence that reproduction of instructions in another medium than they were presented in (i.e. reproduction of an instruction in text if it was offered in pictures or vice versa) is an extra burden on the cognitive load (Seel & Strittmatter, 1989).

If help functions were further integrated into the product user interface, especially if they were completely interactive (meaning that one could perform all tasks through the online help), the user would really have two alternative interfaces, both presented on the screen and in almost identical form (icons, font types, buttons). This might indeed be confusing to some users. Hoek & Kaufman mention this possible 'risk of making it difficult for users to build up a mental model' in their contribution to this volume.

6   Developments
In spite of the risk of confusing users who might develop different mental representations of the same product, user interface designers seem to be convinced that the increasing complexity of new products can only be encountered by further integration of the online help into the product user interface. In their contributions to this volume Hoek & Kaufman from Microsoft and Arcellana & Knabe from Apple Computer clearly represent this point of view.

Hoek & Kaufman notice that 'the effort of using on-line help may badly interrupt the user's workflow'. They describe the efforts that Microsoft has made - and to which they have contributed - to further integrate the help into the product user interface and the problems that accompany such a development. Their article provides an intriguing view of the problems that arise when trying to integrate the help into the product user interface. Hoek & Kaufman show how they try to let the users concentrate on their work, also when they need help. Hoek & Kaufman present the help in such a way that users do not have to switch back and forth between the product interface and the help interface[11].

Knabe describes how Apple Computer has worked towards integration of the help into the product user interface on the basis of John Carroll's minimal manual guidelines, which are based on the learning-by-doing approach. Users should always be encouraged to try out new functions without being afraid of losing track, losing time or losing work. Knabe shows how the Apple Help evolved from answering the 'How do I..?' questions to 'Why don't you..?' Help when the user needs it is one thing; trying to let the user really profit from all functions that may be of use is quite another. Knabe takes the problem that Hoek & Kaufman tackled (integrating the Help in such a way that users can focus on their work, even when they need an answer to a specific question) one step further. He tries to let the users proceed with their work as much as possible and yet makes them interested in discovering new functions.

Arcellana describes the development of the 'Assistants' at Apple Computer as an addition to the 'ordinary' Help (based on Index, Search and Table of Contents). This additional help interface is not so much directed at solving problems presented by the computer, but rather at real-world tasks that the users may have. 'The Assistants were designed to address the user's needs for support of higher level, real world goals, as opposed to lower level, computer based tasks and procedures'. Arcellana also discusses the opportunities to further seduce people into using both the standard and the additional help systems, apart from just trying out the product user interface. He suggests making interfaces for standard and additional help both visually and emotionally more attractive and discusses some ways of doing so.

Especially the elderly users of high-tech products are often reported to have problems with product user interfaces *and* with the additional help[12]. Therefore, it is interesting to focus on this group of users when discussing the integration of help into the product user interface. Would further integration really help the elderly user, or would the possible disadvantages (about which, for instance, Hoek & Kaufman warn) confuse rather than help

---

11   This switching has been described in Jansen & Steehouder (1992) for users who have to fill in forms and by Van Hees (1996) for users of consumer products with manuals.

12   Schriver (1997: p. 507) reports a study of Kelley & Charness (1995) in which they conclude that older adults experience significantly more difficulty in learning to use a computer than younger adults.

the elderly users? Elderly users have been reported to be more careful readers of the additional help than younger users. This may be true for printed manuals, but it remains unclear whether this is also true for online help, as the screen may cause additional problems and because one does have to be somewhat computer-literate to operate an online help facility in the first place.

Bouma describes in minute detail what limitations elderly users may experience - and what should not be considered as limitations of elderly users if the environment were designed adequately. He discusses a wealth of research focussing on the development of suitable interfaces and documents for the elderly. Bouma argues that adaptive user interfaces, based on agent technology, can be especially helpful for this group of users. He stresses the need for designers of both product interfaces and documentation to take elderly consumers more seriously, and to undertake a concerted effort to solve their specific problems in dealing with new technology.

Wright discusses the documentation needs of older people within the context of (1) the evolution in the ways computer users are provided with information and (2) the qualitative changes that have occurred in documentation design. She specifically refers to the question whether all kinds of documents that we have today will still be needed in the future. But as long as additional documentation is still necessary or at least useful, there are three types of document design implications concerning age-associated impairments that have to be taken into account: design implications based on physical needs (sensory limitation), those based on cognitive needs (constraints on mental resources) and those based on emotional needs (personal goals). Wright emphasizes the need for adaptive user interfaces (from which not only elderly users can profit). She also discusses the interdependence of decisions about documentation and the user interface. She stresses that decisions concerning the design of the user interface of a product should not be taken without considering the design of the interface of the documentation and vice versa. This leads to a discussion of the importance of performance-based evaluation during the design process, rather than separate tests for the product user interface and for the documentation[13]. Wright points out that age is not always the most suitable variable for matching between the volunteers assisting with pilot evaluation and the target audience. She stresses that comparable knowledge, experience or interests may be more critical in some contexts.

But why have documentation at all? The need for alternatives, as mentioned by several authors contributing to this book, has been questioned and answered from a historical point of view by *Bouwhuis*. He points out that the reason for being of product

---

13   This conclusion from a researcher must be very valuable for many companies that produce high-tech products: not just the design of the product user interface and document interface seem to be separate tracks in most companies, but the testing of each of these just as well.

documentation can be traced back to perceived weaknesses of spoken communication. Bouwhuis argues that uncertainty is the central problem of users who try to operate products that are new to them using a manual or other kind of help. He also concludes that improvement of this communication process has to be based on a higher degree of integration between the user interface and the documentation.

Problems caused by technology can only be solved by the development of new technology. Problems for users in the operation of new devices, caused by the complexity of all the new features, can only be solved by the development of new and more integrated user interface designs and document designs. The contributions in this volume may be helpful in exploring opportunities for further cooperation among interface designers, document designers and researchers in both fields.

References

- Carroll, J.M. (1990), *The Nurnberg funnel: Designing minimalist instruction for practical computer skill*. Cambridge, MIT Press.
- Hackos, J.T. & Redish, J.C. (1998), *User and task analysis for interface design*. New York, John Wiley & Sons.
- Hees, M.M.W. van (1996), *User instructions for the elderly: what literature tells us*. Journal of technical writing and communication 26, p. 521-536.
- Jansen, C.J.M. & Steehouder, M.F. (1992), *Forms as a source of communication problems*. Journal of technical writing and communication 22, p. 179-194.
- Petersen, D. (1984), *Die Gebrauchsanweisung als kommunikatives Mittel zur Beeinflüssung des Gerätebenutzers Verhaltens* (in German). [The manuals as a means of communication to influence the people's behavior when using products]. Hamburg, Doctoral Thesis.
- Schriver, K.A. (1997): *Dynamics in Document Design*. New York, John Wiley & Sons.
- Seel, N.M. & Strittmatter, P. (1989), *Presentation of information by media and its effect on mental models*. In: H. Mandl, & J.R. Levin, (eds.), Knowledge acquisition from text and pictures. Amsterdam, Elsevier Science Publisher, p. 37-58.
- Wright, P. (1981), *The instructions clearly state... Can't people read?* Applied Ergonomics 12, p. 131-141.

About the authors

Piet Westendorp is a researcher at both Eindhoven University of Technology and Delft University of Technology. He has published several books and many articles concerning instructions for use. Moreover, he has worked as a freelance journalist, technical communicator and advisor for many major companies. His most recent book is *Open here: the art of instructional design* (together with Paul Mijksenaar; Thames & Hudson, 1999).

Carel Jansen holds the chair of Business Communication at Nijmegen University. He has published books and papers about optimizing the order of instructions, intercultural aspects of technical communication, and the design of instructional documents, specifically government forms and software manuals.

Rob Punselie is a creative consultant for major commercial and nonprofit organizations. He specializes in content and writing for the web and has published frequently on this subject, including his book *Wijzer op het web* ('Wiser on the web', Samsom, 1999). He is also President of the Netherlands Society for Technical Information and Communication (STIC).

Help yourself: designing help to fit software users and their work

Tjeerd Hoek[@]
Leah Kaufman[@]

Summary

Well-designed software allows users to focus their attention, as needed, on their tasks instead of the application. However, when users need help with unfamiliar tasks, the effort of using on-line help may badly interrupt the user's workflow. Our work on the MS-Office help system has continually focused on integrating help and the application interface, aiming to ultimately merge the help system with the interface - when you need help, you don't have to go far from your work to get it. This paper discusses issues addressed in the design of on-line help for each release of MS-Office, focusing on design changes that improve how on-line help fits within the context of the users' work.

1   Bringing help closer to the user

What irks people about using software? In a 1997 focus group study conducted at Microsoft, we asked experienced computer users to tell us about aspects of software that feel 'bloated'. While their responses varied from hardware performance to the problems of upgrading, one of the most frequent responses was: 'Help - when I can't find the topic I am looking for and I know it has to be in there somewhere. It feels like I spend hours trying to find the one thing I need.' Each of the study's participants related similar stories: needing help for a particular task; going to the on-line help for assistance, and spending an unexpectedly large amount of time in Help instead of on the task they had originally planned to do. These selfreports are supported by observations from our lab tests and site visits where users who want help for an unfamiliar task may wander further and further away from their work as they struggle to locate, recognize, and use the appropriate on-line help topic. While any workday may be filled with interruptions - phone calls, meetings, and the like - delays at the computer, especially ones that feel avoidable such as getting help, appear to be a major source of frustration for software users. Sellen and Nicol (1990) agree with this assessment:

@   tjeerdh@microsoft.com
@   leahk@uswest.net

Finding the simplest piece of information can turn into a complicated exercise
[...] If and when we find what we need it will probably take a long time to get
back to the task we were working on, if we can remember what it was.

In any situation, a good tool extends some human strength or ability, and a particularly
excellent tool may work so well you don't even notice it's being used. When we design
software tools, we imagine that if the software is good enough, the computer might
'disappear' and almost all your attention can focus on the work. Although it is normal to pay
attention when learning or practicing a task, when you consistently halt your work in order
to adjust the tool or figure it out, much of the tool's utility vanishes. We want users to stay
focused on their tasks instead of on figuring out how to do the task with the software.
Although learning to use the software or a particular feature invariably takes time away
from one's work, locating the information you need should still be quick and efficient.

What does this imply about help systems? That beyond periods when users choose to take
the time to learn something with a tutorial or help topic, help needs to support people when
they interrupt their work to figure out or remind themselves how to do a particular task. This
approach builds on the principles of minimalist instruction introduced by John M. Carroll in
The Nurnberg Funnel (1990). In the first principle 'Choose an action-oriented approach',
Van der Meij & Carroll (1998) emphasize the need to balance the user's desire to act with the
knowledge necessary for the action - that is, when the user wants to act, make sure the
necessary information is available. One of the hallmarks of minimalist instruction is that the
priority in design should be 'to provide users with an immediate opportunity to act
meaningfully.'

Our designs for help in MS-Office try to follow this principle, and in every release of MS-
Office we have come closer to integrating help with the application in a way that both
minimizes the amount of interruption and maximizes the amount of time the user focuses
on his or her work. Each version has its own issues and problems, but when viewed across
the four different versions described below, it is clear that our interface design work over
the past eight years has focused on bringing help closer to the users and their work.

2   Help in the first Microsoft Office suite

Early on-line help systems mimicked the large manuals that usually accompanied the
software; they featured an Index and a Table of Contents as the primary routes to the help
content. Users relied on two methods for locating a particular help topic: scrolling through
the list until you found the one you wanted or using 'Find' to locate a topic containing a
specific word. Perhaps the biggest drawback of the system was that the users needed to
know the exact words for describing the task or the actual name of the feature they wanted

to use. Only by using the application's jargon or 'computerese' would a user succeed in finding the right help topic. Even the Index, which aimed to assist users by suggesting appropriate search terms, failed to really address the problem; users had trouble proposing an initial word to start with. The time and effort needed to recall a term and spent scrolling through a seemingly endless index made going to on-line help in these applications a distinctly separate task from doing one's work.

3   Help in Office 95

When we began work on Office 95, we recognized that the solution to this problem required a help system where people could use their own words for describing a task or feature, instead of recalling specific terms that the computer could recognize. The idea of using 'natural language' with computers is well established; it is often an integral part of descriptions of easy computer use. For example, in *The Trouble with Computers*, Thomas Landauer (1995) describes a fictitious computer-based 'Home shopping supermall' where users can

> ...scan the listings, categories, and ads, just as now. But pick a listing or an ad
> and up comes a description...Better than that, you can search. Type a phrase:
> 'dentist with an opening today,' 'Levi jeans size 33/36', 'broccoli and feta cheese
> pizza by the slice.'

In this example, people search the 'Supermall' using colloquial phrases; they use words and terms that they already know for describing the item they want. Our desire to improve help by allowing people to use their own words dovetailed with Microsoft's research into natural language and led to the development and implementation of the 'Answer Wizard' - a natural language technology embedded in the help system that associates colloquial terms with appropriate help topics.

Instead of searching through an index and trying to match 'computerese' terms to their tasks, people could use their own words for describing what they want to do. Ideally, the help system would recognize these terms and associate them with an appropriate Help topic. This first version of the Answer Wizard gave users a traditional entry field for typing in their question (see figure 1).

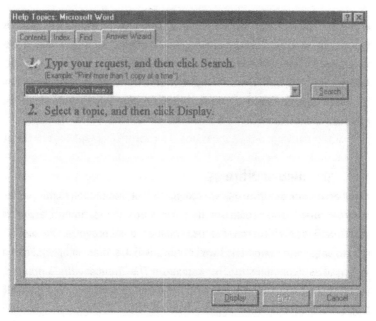

Figure 1.
The Office 95 Answer Wizard dialog box.

The Answer Wizard then uses a network of synonyms, terms, and relationships between the terms and help topics to identify the topics most closely associated with the words in the user's question. This network is built on the terms that MS-Office application specialists and usability experts continually collect from users' Help questions. One part of their task is to assign associations and probability of association 'weights' between these thousands of terms and the areas in the application that evoke those questions. The Answer Wizard assesses the terms in a user's query. It determines which topics to display by considering each term and then identifying the help topics which have the most terms linked at the strongest probabilities.

The advantage of the Answer Wizard system is that different descriptions of a given task all yield the same appropriate help topic. For example, entering any of these three queries in MS-Word 'make the letters more noticeable', 'bold my text', and 'dark letters' will bring up a list of help topics that includes the choice 'Apply bold formatting to text or numbers'.[1]

Our usability research shows that this natural language interface can have a distinct advantage over the more standard keyword index. For example, in a usability test with ten novice and intermediate Word users we found that all the participants located help for

1   More details about Microsoft research on Bayesian nets and the Answer Wizard technology can be found at
      http://research.microsoft.com/~horvitz/lum.htm.

unfamiliar tasks faster and more comfortably by using the Answer Wizard than using the index. The participants explained that it was frustrating to '...think along the lines of the person who wrote the program'. From their perspective, the Answer Wizard was preferable because they did not need to know the exact terms for their tasks or spend time tracking down the correct keywords. One participant neatly summed this up: "I don't feel like I'm hunting for the right word. It's like I can type in what I'm seeking and what it means to me and the computer's gonna look for that. I like that feature". We also found that connecting the users' terms with the help topics can build an association between the users' words and the 'computerese' terms handled in the application. For example, when users see that their phrase 'make the second line of my paragraph indent further than the first' the on-line help takes them to 'Examples of paragraph indentation' and 'hanging indent', they learn the computer's way of describing the task[2].

Although the Answer Wizard and natural language technology was introduced with the release of Office 95, it did not immediately improve how people used the on-line help. The user interface to search for help topics appeared in the middle of the screen, covering up the user's work. This meant that the initial experience with the user interface for help took place outside of the user's work, contributing to the sense that going to Help is like starting a different application, forcing you to leave the context of your work.
In addition, many users continued to rely on the more familiar Index and Table of Contents search mechanisms. From continued usability testing we learned that the user interface did not communicate to the user how to best use the Answer Wizard. Despite our efforts to encourage users to type in phrases rather than single words, people tended to treat it exactly like the keyword search mechanism of traditional help systems, typing in one-word queries instead of the more verbose, task or goal oriented questions for which the Answer Wizard was optimized. Even when we placed an example of the colloquial phrases that the Answer Wizard could understand at the first instruction, the problem remained. The result was that users did not perceive the Answer Wizard UI as any different from, or more useful than, traditional search UI for help systems. Hence, the natural language technology was largely undiscovered and underused.

How could we increase the usage of the natural language technology compared to the usage of other search mechanisms, such as Contents, Index, and Keyword Search? How could we encourage users to take full advantage of the technology by just using their own words to describe what they wanted to do? Could we make the Answer Wizard UI more

---

2   The accuracy of the Answer Wizard is about 80%, i.e. in 80% of the cases in our tests the 'correct' help topic is in fact in the first set of (5) returned hits (topics) displayed in the balloon by the Assistant (tests done with Office 97). The total success rate of users using Help is of course lower, since users still need to find that topic in the list, recognize it as a potential answer to their problem, click on it and read it, and then hopefully actually be helped by the content of the topic. On average, Help is successful for users about 50% of the time.

accessible and integrated with the users' tasks? Our work to solve these problems led to the research into social user interfaces - an approach involving animated, cartoon-like characters which may engage users in a more social interaction and build a rapport with them - and the subsequent development of the Office Assistant character interface in MS-Office 97.

4   Help in Office 97

Although the UI changes to the MS-Office 95 Answer Wizard had improved the usability of help, it did not make the Answer Wizard more discoverable and it failed to change the user's preferred method for doing a search based on single keywords. We believed that if users could more easily discover the Answer Wizard, they would be more likely to use it in favor of other search methods, spend less time and effort looking for help, and even improve their vocabulary for computer-based tasks.

To improve discoverability and invite users to search by describing their tasks, we changed the Answer Wizard interface from the standard dialog box to a 'social' user interface consisting of an animated Office Assistant and a balloon window for communicating with the user (see figure 2).

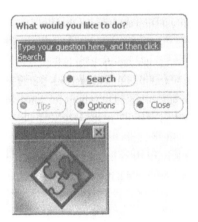

Figure 2.
In Office 97, the Office Assistant presents the Answer Wizard's interface.

When the user clicks on the Office Assistant, the 'balloon' displays the question 'What would you like to do?' rather than a 'What term do you want to search for?' type of question. After the users type in their question or goal, the same balloon displays a set of suggested help topics that match the user's query. With this design solution, we have put the entry point for on-line help directly in the context of the user's document, thus making help immediately accessible.

The help design work for MS-Office 97 also provided solutions to other problems found in previous releases; for example, providing help the first time a user does an unfamiliar task; improving the Answer Wizard's ability to locate the correct help topic; making the presentation of tips less obtrusive; and putting more information into system error messages. We could now offer help in the context of a task that is 'new' to the user. When users do something for the first time they may need explanatory information. Later on, when they are familiar with the feature, the help won't be as necessary. In Office 97, the first time that a user selects a command such as 'Pivot Table' or 'Mail Merge', the Assistant asks if they would like help on using the feature. So that information they might need is being offered within the context of the their work. It also means the user doesn't have to go hunting through help to locate the information; help brings it right to the user instead.

Finally, MS-Office 95 displays tips or suggestions, cued by the user's actions, proposing alternative use of the software in a narrow window directly underneath the toolbars. For example, the help system could monitor for particular actions such as cutting and pasting in Excel and present a tip recommending that the user try to 'drag and drop' instead. However, many users disliked the amount of screen space taken up by the tip bar and found the constant changes in this part of the screen distracting. To fix these problems, we changed the cue for tip availability in MS-Office 97 to a light bulb that appears next to the Office Assistant. This design solution provided a much less obtrusive means of giving non-critical advice to users about how to use the software in potentially more effective and efficient ways.

5   Help in Office 2000

Office 2000 gave us the opportunity to tackle a large set of outstanding UI help design issues from MS-Office 97.

First, the lack of integration between the Assistant search UI and the help topic display window: the Assistant was designed to be part of the application while Help was built separately. Since the Assistant was designed to disappear when a non-Office program was being used on screen (because it has no help to offer for other programs), it also hides itself when help appears. This means that when the user clicked on a help topic from the list in the Office Assistant's balloon, the help topic would appear while the Assistant would disappear, taking the list of possible help topics with it. If the user now wants to try another topic from the returned list, they need to go back to the Assistant, re-open the help balloon and click the 'search' button again to perform the same search. The users must then choose a new topic, which is different from the topic chosen before (if they can remember which one that was, since this is not made obvious visually). Hence, there is no way to efficiently browse through a list of potentially relevant help topics and quickly check out the contents of each one.

Second, once a help topic is selected, the actual help content is displayed in a separate window that completely overlays the user's work area. Although the window is resizable, its default size is determined by the contents, and the window does not 'remember' its size after a user changed it. If the help topic contains many lines of text, the help window displays all of it (see figure 3). This literally puts the help contents outside of the context of the user's work and can sometimes actually cover the document completely:

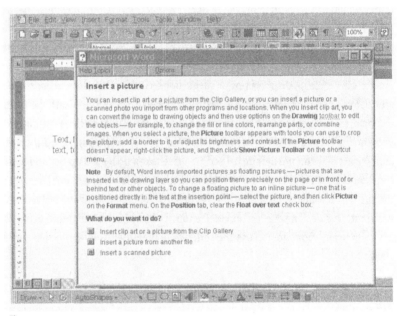

Figure 3.
In Office 97, Help Topics can obscure the user's document.

The users must choose whether the help or their document should receive the focus of their attention. This presentation reinforces the notion that help is 'a different place' making it difficult for users to perform the tasks described in the help topic in the application itself. In our usability tests, users would often read all the information in a help topic and then close it to return to the application. Trying to remember the information they just read, they would attempt to perform the steps necessary to accomplish their task. In many cases they would find out half way through that they had forgotten some of the steps, and they would have to repeat their search for that very same help topic they had just dismissed.

For Office 2000, our goal was to come up with a design that gave users a better balance between the information provided in help, and the contents and functionality in their document window. To accomplish this we devised a separate pane that displays the help content while keeping the majority of the user's workspace visible (see figure 4).

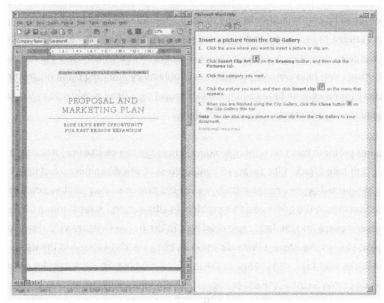

Figure 4.
The Office 2000 Help window displays topics alongside the user's document.

This allows the Office Assistant, the search results, and the help window to share the screen with the application window. The help content is docked to the side of the screen next to, rather than floating over, the user's work. This configuration makes it easier for users to read the topic's description of the steps in the task and perform them in the application. The Assistant stays visible and out of the way. If the user has the balloon open with a list of possible topics visible, clicking each topic makes its contents appear in the pane. Users no longer have to switch back and forth between the help window and the application window to check out several topics.

This resolves a myriad of design problems and, in particular, reduces the user's cognitive load. Users are no longer forced to close the help and rely on remembering the procedural steps to do the task within their workspace. It also means a lower cost for quickly checking out a potentially useful help topic, because users can easily toggle between the different help topics, quickly reviewing the contents until they find the one that suits their task.

The Office 2000 on-line help design also addressed several other issues. For example, the browsing experience in the help content tended to be broken or confusing to users. The navigation controls for the help window were not consistent with standardized browser navigation controls. For example, the 'Back' button was not always available to users and did not always function as anticipated. Navigation controls lacked a 'Forward' button, so users could not recover from clicking one 'Back' too many. Also, because each help topic determined its own window size and location, the experience of browsing through different topics tended to be 'jumpy' and unpredictable, with help content, navigation controls and the window itself often ending up in places on the screen where users did not want them. The Office 2000 help window solved these problems by adopting standardized browser controls for navigation between topics, and providing a fixed window so as to always display the help content in the same location.

Another problem was that although natural language can be used to formulate a question, the list of help topics still appears in 'computerese'. Even when the correct help topic is in the list returned by the Answer Wizard, we noticed that users may still have trouble identifying the correct topic. We addressed this problem in Office 2000 by substituting the terms from the user's query into the help topic displayed in the Answer Wizard's list. For example, if a generic topic in the Answer Wizard's list is a strong match to a term in the user's query, the term in the help topic can change to the user's own words. So if the user for example types 'How do I draw a cloud', the list of suggested help topics will include 'Add a cloud'. Although the actual help topic title is 'Add an Auto shape, circle or square', the substitution is easier for the user to recognize and still points the user to the appropriate help topic.

Also, our in-house research has continually assessed the accuracy of the Answer Wizard database as it went through each product release. Our goal is for users to type in a query and get a reasonable, recognizable help topic within the top five choices offered by the Answer Wizard. Although the system has not yet reached this standard, our continued work on the Answer Wizard contents and organization has improved its accuracy in returning appropriate help topics. When we compare the performance of an early version of the Answer Wizard with the latest release of MS-Office 97, the results show a large improvement: the frequency with which the correct help topic appears in the Answer Wizard's 5 item 'hit list' rose from 47% to 77%. As we continue to refine the database of terms and relationships, we hope to come even closer to providing users with the information they need most for the task at hand, fulfilling the basic principle of minimalist instruction by making sure that the information is available.

6   The future of help - user interface integration

Our work to date is part of an on-going effort in software design that emphasizes a close fit between the software and the user's work. We hope that eventually users will be able to switch smoothly between a minimal interface, one that is optimized for efficiently completing common tasks, and a more explanatory interface optimized for discovering and learning new functionality.

Our continuing work towards this goal focuses on two related areas. First, we are testing and studying improved interfaces which use speech recognition and interactive voice systems. With speech recognition systems, particularly command-control systems with agents that can execute larger goals, users may be able to tell the computer to perform their tasks. Users could choose whether the system executes the command on its own or teaches them how to do it. Second, by capturing user actions we can learn how to make the UI adapt to the user's goals. If we become better at understanding the actions and decisions that comprise users' tasks, we may be able to create a profile for any user. A dynamic profile composed of an individual user's goals, interests and preferences, ways of working, and skill level, may enable us to accurately and continuously adapt the UI and help system to the user's needs, offering appropriate information where necessary. In the Microsoft Office 2000 products we are taking the first steps towards a UI that adapts to the way an individual uses the product - for example, menus and toolbars are continuously modified depending on usage over time - and it is likely that we will continue our efforts in that direction. Great care will have to be taken over the introduction of such UI mechanisms, as there is a risk of making it difficult for users to build a mental model of how the UI works. Similar issues arise with the increased use of context sensitive UI's, and the design of these adaptive and context sensitive systems will require careful consideration, to make sure the product remains predictable and intuitive to users.

References

- Carroll, J.M. (1990), *The Nurnberg funnel: designing minimalist instruction for practical computer skill*. Cambridge, MIT Press.
- Landauer, T.K. (1995), *The trouble with computers: usefulness, usability, and productivity.* Cambridge, MIT Press.
- Sellen, A. & Nicol, A. (1990), Building user-centered on-line help. In: B. Laurel (ed.), *The art of human-computer interface design*. Reading, Addison-Wesley.
- Van der Meij, H. & Carroll, J.M. (1998), Principles and heuristics for designing minimalist instruction. In: Carroll, J.M. (ed.), *Minimalism beyond the Nurnberg funnel*. Cambridge, MIT Press.

About the authors

Tjeerd Hoek studied Industrial Design Engineering at the Delft University of Technology where he received his masters degree cum laude in 1992. He joined Microsoft Corporation in 1994, to work as a product designer on networked office devices, such as digital copiers, phones and faxes. After this he worked for several years on the interaction design of the Microsoft Office suite of products, where he was responsible for main areas of the core user interface and directed conceptual projects exploring the future of productivity software. Tjeerd is currently the lead for user interface design in the Windows User Experience team at Microsoft.

Leah Kaufman received her graduate training in cognitive psychology at the University of Washington in Seattle. From 1992-1999 she worked as a usability engineer at Microsoft and conducted usability research on more than twenty different software and hardware products, including the user interface and help systems for MS-Office 2000.

Designing online help for the Mac OS

Kevin Knabe@

Summary

The online help system included with the Mac OS 8.5 was the product of a decade of research and development at Apple into how users can work most effectively with online help. At first the team focused on developing a help system optimally designed for answering procedural ('How do I...?') questions. Later they would broaden the scope of the help to better support goal formation and error recovery. They would also switch from a proprietary help technology to HTML, to assure wider adoption by application developers. The new approach was strongly influenced by the principles of minimalist documentation, along with an ongoing process of iterative design and usability testing. This article summarizes the design efforts and presents a general set of guidelines for help writers and designers.

1   The evolution of online help for the Mac OS

1.1   Early research

Online help for the Mac OS began to take shape in 1988 when Apple's Human Interface Group reviewed the available literature on help, evaluated existing help systems, and conducted videotaped observations of user behavior. In several studies, users were observed thinking aloud while doing tasks in application programs. The team found that users tended to represent problems in the form of questions, and that questions fell into five general categories:

- goal-oriented questions ('What can I do with this?')
- descriptive questions ('What is this?')
- procedural questions ('How do I do this?')
- interpretive questions ('Why did that happen?')
- navigational questions ('Where am I?')

Additionally, they found that most questions were either descriptive ('What is...?') or procedural ('How do I...?').

@   kknabe@cdnow.com

Based on these findings, the designers proposed a system for asking and answering questions. A user would begin by choosing a question type, such as 'What is...?' or 'How do I...?' from the Help menu. Though this menu design was never fully implemented, two of the menu items eventually became part of the system. 'What is...?' help took the form of Balloon Help, which was released with Mac OS 7.0. 'How do I...?' help took the form of Apple Guide.

1.2   The design of Apple Guide

User testing of the Macintosh Electronic Reference - a HyperCard-based online reference for the Mac OS - demonstrated many of the problems with traditional forms of online documentation. When users accessed help, they switched out of the context for doing a task. To follow the steps in the help, users had to repeatedly switch windows or else read and remember the entire sequence of steps. Users often skipped steps, performed steps incorrectly, or failed to branch appropriately on conditional instructions (Knabe, 1995).

Apple Guide was designed to address the problem of layer switching. When users access help in Apple Guide, they stay in the active application. Instructions are presented in small system windows that float on top of everything else on the screen so that help is never covered. The instruction panels present one step at a time, so that instructions are small and unlikely to cover the functional interface. The user pages from one step to the next. The help is able to skip steps that the user has already completed and present remediation when the user gets off track.

Another common problem with traditional online help is that users are confused by pictures of interface elements. They often click the pictures, mistaking them for functional interface elements. Rather than showing illustrations of objects on screen, Apple Guide points out the actual object by drawing a bright red circle (known as a *coachmark*) around the object, as in figure 1.

Apple Guide had a standard set of information access features. A user could access help by choosing an item from the help menu. They could look up a specific help topic by using a table of contents, an alphabetical index, or a keyword search feature.

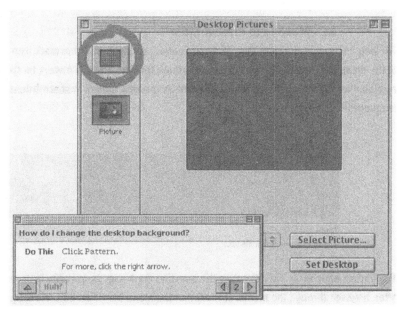

Figure 1.
An Apple Guide panel along with a 'coachmark' circling a button.

1.3   Usability testing and market research

Product teams conducted usability tests of help content as it was developed. Typically these tests would involve recruiting six to eight participants and having them think aloud while performing tasks with developmental software. Participants were encouraged to use the online help whenever they encountered a task that was unfamiliar.

Usability testing helped identify a variety of problems. These included: problems with the grouping of tasks in the table of contents; inadequate search keywords; problems with the naming of individual tasks; use of unfamiliar vocabulary; and the use of panels that were too big. Generally, instructional designers were able to address these problems in rewrites. Market research indicated fairly low levels of usage and satisfaction. In focus groups, users complained that Apple Guide presented information too slowly and in inadequate depth. Although Apple Guide has been optimally designed to 'spoon feed' the correct instructions to users, many users - particularly experienced users - didn't want to be spoon fed. They wanted a more in-depth body of content that supported faster information access.

2   Design goals for online help in Mac OS 8.5

The experience of designing and testing Apple Guide helped inform the design of the next generation of help. In designing help for Mac OS 8.5, the designers sought to preserve the strengths of the existing system while addressing the known problems.

2.1 Make help discoverable

The help menu introduced in Mac OS 7.0 appeared as a small question mark icon at the right of the menu bar. This design was chosen to assure that there would always be space available for the menu, even in applications with complex menus in space-intensive languages such as German (see figure 2).

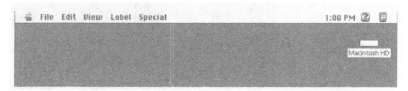

Figure 2.
The Help menu in Mac OS 7.0.

Many users apparently did not notice the question mark icon. In usability tests, participants often browsed through the menus at the left of the menu bar - File, Edit, View, Special - then stopped exploring. Some participants didn't use the menu even after they were prompted to look for Help. Discoverability was identified as the number one usability problem with the help system, because for many users, it was the *only* problem they ever encountered.

In Mac OS 8.0, an obvious solution was implemented; the menu was moved to the left and labeled 'Help'. Placing the menu on the path of exploratory learning, has led to a noticeable increase in the discoverability and usage of help (see figure 3).

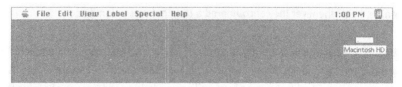

Figure 3.
The Help menu in Mac OS 8.0.

2.2 Make help easy to author

Apple Guide was not widely adopted by Macintosh application developers, partly because of the difficulty in scripting Apple Guide databases in the absence of a dedicated authoring tool. Also, many developers didn't want to develop altogether separate versions of help for the Macintosh and Windows versions of their applications. It was clear that HTML was becoming the standard for authoring online information. It had become equally clear that the help for Mac OS should be HTML based. This would allow authors to use any of the available HTML authoring tools. It would also allow straightforward porting of help content between the Mac OS and Windows.

2.3 Provide a central point of access to all available help

In Mac OS 8.5, all help for the Mac OS - procedural and non-procedural, local and web-based - is available through a central point of access. All of the help is accessed through an application called Help Viewer, which pulls together a variety of help technologies. The Help Viewer lets users display and browse content written in HTML, perform full-text searches of HTML content on the hard disk, launch Apple Guide sequences for step-by-step guidance through complex procedures, open a web browser to a specific URL, and run scripts to automate tasks (see figure 4).

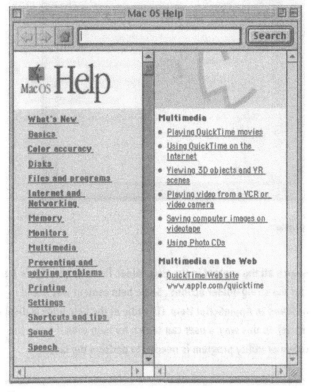

Figure 4.
The table of contents for Mac OS 8.5 Help, displayed in the Help Viewer.

The Help Viewer can also display a page listing all available help 'books'. This page, known as the Help Center, is assembled dynamically based on the contents of the Help folder. (An application developer can have help appear in the Help Center by installing a folder of HTML files in the Help folder and including special meta-tags in one of the files.) The user can thus browse among all of the content in the Help folder, not just find help for a single application (see figure 5).

Figure 5.
The Help Center.

The user can also search all the content in the Help folder. For example, figure 6 shows the results of a search for the string 'folder actions'. Some help content was found in Mac OS Help, and some was found in AppleScript Help. (The title of the help book is displayed next to the title of the article). In this way, a user can search for help even if he or she doesn't know which application or utility program is needed to perform the task.

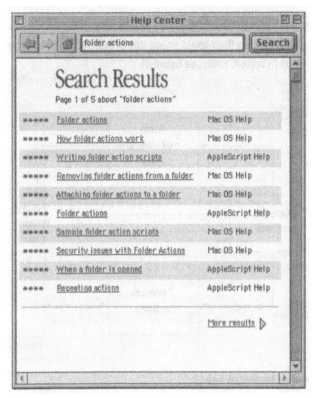

Figure 6.
The results of a search.

2.4 Take advantage of the Internet

In phone surveys, a segment of users requested more comprehensive technical information.
A great deal of this information had already been developed and was already available on
Apple's website. For instance, the Tech Info Library contained over ten thousand articles
written by Apple's Customer Support Division. It was therefore possible to vastly increase
the volume of content in the help system by simply linking to the existing content on the
Web. (Notice in figure 4 that one of the links is to the QuickTime website).

2.5 Define tasks broadly

In writing Apple Guide sequences or other forms of step-by-step procedures, writers tended
to approach a task as merely a series of actions (as in figure 7).

Figure 7.
A linear task model.

If users were robots, this approach would probably be effective. In reality, users are constantly forming goals, refining their goals, trying things out, seeing what happens, and deciding what to do next (Norman, 1988; see figure 8).

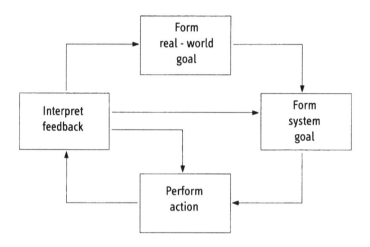

Figure 8.
A broader, more iterative task model.

To fully support tasks, online help should assist users in forming goals, performing actions, and interpreting feedback. This represents a shift in instructional philosophy that places somewhat less emphasis on procedural instruction, while placing greater emphasis on presenting the rationale for doing a task and on interpreting feedback in troubleshooting scenarios.

2.6 Write minimally

Although writers were encouraged to take a broad view of tasks, they were also encouraged to write about only those aspects of the task that users were unlikely to figure out through exploratory learning (Carroll, 1990). In usability testing of Apple Guide content, writers saw that some tasks could always be done without help. Figure 9 shows one such example. Apple CD Audio Player, an application for playing audio CDs on a Macintosh, includes help for playing a CD. In five rounds of testing with over forty participants, no one was unable to do this task without help. In other words, no one ever needed the instructions shown in figure 9.

Figure 9.
Example of unnecessary instructions.

Figure 10 shows an example of the same task documented in the new approach. At first glance, the minimalist approach may seem long. Keep in mind, though, that figure 9 shows only one of several screens that the user must page through, whereas figure 10 shows the whole task. Note that the procedural aspect of the task is handled in just one sentence. Most of the help is actually devoted to troubleshooting.

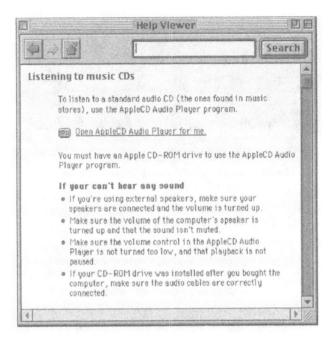

Figure 10.
Example of a minimalist approach.

2.7   Automate tasks whenever possible

Notice also in figure 10 that a button is provided for automatically opening Apple CD Audio
Player. These 'do it for me' buttons are used throughout the help, usually to open the
window or dialog box that must be used to perform a task. The use of automation is limited
to tasks that are scriptable within an application, and which do not require user input.
When part of a task is automated, users tend to complete the task more quickly and with
fewer errors. Although this approach goes against much conventional pedagogical wisdom,
we have found that many users are willing to sacrifice learning in the interests of fast and
successful task completion. We have also found that users can learn from an automated
approach to a task; user test participants who rely on automation to complete a task at the
beginning of a session often can complete identical or similar tasks without help at the end
of the session.

3   Conclusions

The new approach has performed remarkably well in the usability lab. In one study, users
completed tasks successfully in 21 of the 23 cases in which they used help (that is, after
exploratory learning had failed). The core elements of the system, troubleshooting - focused
writing, task automation, and the use of step-by-step guidance when appropriate, appear to
support users well 'when all else fails'. Apple plans to continue research into how well the
new help system approach is accepted by developers and users in the field.

References

- Carroll, J.M. (1990), *The Nurnberg funnel: designing minimalist instruction for practical computer skill.* Cambridge, MIT Press.
- Norman, D.A. (1988), *The design of everyday things,* New York, Doubleday.
- Knabe, K.J. (1995), *Apple Guide: A Case Study in User-Aided Design of Online Help.* In: CHI'95 Conference companion on human factors in computing systems, p. 286-287.

Acknowledgements

The information in this paper was gathered primarily from Apple internal technical reports. The author would like to acknowledge the people who contributed to those reports: Kate Gomoll, Tom Gomoll, Rachel Haas, Jeffrey Herman, Jeremy Hewes, Glenn Katz, Kristy Knabe, Gordon Meyer, Anne Nicol, Jim Palmer, Abigail Sellen, Mike Thompson, John Trumble, and Irene Wong.

About the author

Kevin Knabe manages the user interface design group at CDNOW (www.cdnow.com), a music e-commerce site based near Philadelphia. Previously he worked at Apple Computer, IBM, and Sun Microsystems. His work at Apple spanned ten years, first as a technical writer, then as a usability specialist and interface designer. He was the lead interface designer for the Mac OS 8.5 online help system. Kevin holds a Master of Arts in Professional Writing from Carnegie Mellon University.

Designing Assistants

José Arcellana@

Summary

Assistants in version 8.0 onwards of the Macintosh system software represent the currently most evolved form of on-line help on Macintosh. They were designed to address users' needs for support of higher-level, real-world goals, as opposed to lower-level, computer-based tasks and procedures. Assistants are designed to transfer as much of the burden of achieving user goals as possible from the user to the computer. They minimize the cognitive load associated with understanding and recalling computer-based procedures and tasks. At the same time, they create an affective environment that tries to be reassuring and trustworthy. As part of this drive to minimize the load on the user, Assistants are deliberately underdesigned, using the simplest of user interface elements. A possible future direction might be to enrich the affective aspects with more visually appealing graphics, more emotional content in the language, and other techniques - without compromising their effectiveness.

1   Introduction

An 'assistant' as described in this paper is a specific type of application program that was designed and developed as part of Apple Computer's Macintosh system software (version 8.0 and later), and there are some important differences between this and similar programs, such as wizards and agents. Further, Assistants do not have any 'artificial intelligence' in the sense that the term has been commonly understood. Assistants are part of a spectrum of Macintosh system software on-line help components ranging from balloons to assistants:

- balloons and tool tips (answer the question 'What is this?')
- traditional, text-based, read-only, on-line help ('How do I do this?')
- guided task sequences ('Show and tell me how')
- automated steps and procedures ('Do it for me')
- Assistants ('Do it for me and spare me the details')

This range starts from simpler, more direct information and steps through to more complex and indirect task execution. Each component is designed to support specific end-user goals related to using a computer, and their interfaces are optimized (even simplified) to support

@   arcellana@alumni.stanford.org

those goals. As examples, this paper uses the Mac OS Setup Assistant and the Internet Setup Assistant, which were shipped with the Macintosh OS 8.0 system software (see figure 1).

Figure 1.
The Assistants that shipped with Macintosh system software, version 8.0.

2   Why an Assistant?

Assistants were designed to fill a usability gap in software, especially system software. Because user interfaces tend to be optimized for high-frequency tasks (opening a file on your hard disk, for example), support for common real-world goals that involve performing very low-frequency tasks, such as setting up your computer for the first time, or setting up Internet access, has been missing.

Accomplishing higher-level goals, such as setting up your computer, usually involves interacting with disparate parts of the user interface, some of which are fairly complex and difficult to use (mostly because their design has not been optimized for frequent use; infrequent use, unfortunately, is often an excuse for sub-optimal design).

Assistants are best suited to supporting users in accomplishing complex, infrequent, yet common real-world goals (as distinct from computer tasks) that involve disparate user interface elements and difficult procedural steps that are seldom done but need to be done by most users at some time. The complexity and infrequency of such goals make it harder for users to remember the tasks involved and the steps required to accomplish those tasks; an Assistant in such cases is quite useful and has a high perceived value.

When complex but infrequent goals are attempted only by a small minority of users, however, the design and development costs required to create and ship an Assistant often cannot be justified by its limited target user population. In such cases, highly detailed, comprehensive, and well-written user documentation is a more cost-efficient solution. The obvious examples of complex and infrequent goals are setting up a new version of the operating system, an application program, Internet access or a new hardware device. Such goals also include diagnostics and troubleshooting. (Macintosh system software version 8.0 shipped with two Assistants: the Macintosh Setup Assistant and the Internet Setup Assistant.) Assistants are unnecessary for goals that are relatively simple, frequent, and uncommon, because most users will not want to deal with the interface overhead that an Assistant brings in such cases - primarily, the construct of an interview. For example, most people will not want to go through an interview that asks them what time it is when all they want to do is set the time. Also, users tend to remember the steps involved in accomplishing tasks that they do frequently, because they get a lot of practice and so are less likely to need an Assistant or even find one useful.

3   Alternatives to Assistants

In the process of designing Assistants, a couple of alternatives were considered as ways to fill the same usability gap that Assistants were meant to fill. Given the design goals, the tendencies that evolved were either to integrate the disparate user interface elements into a single, comprehensive, self-contained user interface, or to break down the elements into more discrete, separate, cognitively digestible chunks.

3.1   Combination control panels

The first tendency, to bring together the otherwise disparate, scattered user interface elements into a unified collection, resulted in a prototype design for a setup control panel. This single control panel included controls that enabled users to set the date and time, name their computer, set their password, set their local preferences for text and number formats and paper size, and so on. (A *control panel* is a small application program that presents a single window containing controls and other user interface elements designed, typically, to enable users to set values for system-wide settings).

While the prototype design succeeded in bringing together the different user interface elements into one place, it failed to support the design and real-world end-user goals in several important ways. Consider a situation in which it is better for a user to set location before paper size. This is a 'preferred sequence' in accomplishing a high-level goal.

A combination control panel could not suggest such a sequence, beyond a layout that positioned controls that should be set first closer to the top and to the left which in many cases would have to be flopped, that is, mirrored to the right, in languages that use right-to-left writing systems. Further, the combination control panel by itself, without using on-line help or some other, separate and additional mechanism, could not explain to users why these different user interface elements are grouped together and how to use them. This separate help mechanism added a layer of complexity that worked against the design goal, making the combination control panel seem less assistive than it actually is.

3.2   Staggered dialog boxes

The second tendency, to break down or deconstruct the disparate user interface elements involved and to present their pieces in some logical sequence, resulted in 'staggered dialog boxes'. These staggered user interfaces solved the problem of sequencing that the combination control panel could not address, but they did not help users understand why the controls were being presented in the order that they were, or how best to set the controls that were presented - again, without some external, additional mechanism such as on-line help, which adds complexity and runs counter to the design goals. Further, staggered dialog boxes fail to hide computer-level tasks from the user because they simply break down the user interface elements in what may be smaller pieces but are not necessarily any more understandable just because they are in smaller pieces. In other words, a field that is labeled 'DNS' with no other explanation is inscrutable whether it is by itself or part of a larger set of other controls that are similarly labeled. As the limitations of those two design tendencies became apparent, the Assistants' design evolved towards a balance between them, as described in the next section.

4   What is an Assistant?

In its simplest terms, an Assistant forms a goal-oriented layer of interaction between users and the 'usual' interface by grouping computer-based tasks and representing them to users in terms of a real-world goal. An Assistant does the following.

• Executes computer tasks in support of a single real-world end-user goal
Most users do not use computers for their own sake. Most users use computers because there is something they want to do that could perhaps be better or more easily done using a computer.
An Assistant attempts to identify a single, fairly high-level, real-world goal ('I want to get on the Internet') and then gathers the different user interface widgets and components that support that goal, presenting them to users in a logical manner (see figure 2).

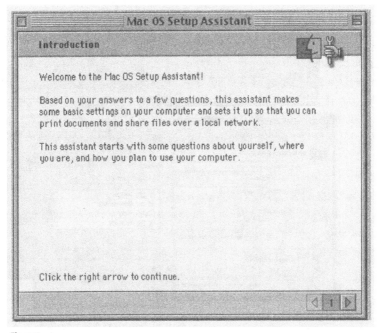

Figure 2.
The Mac OS Setup Assistant introduces itself and confirms which goal it is designed to support.

• Augments (does not replace) the primary interface
  Because it is both impossible and undesirable to predict every use of an user interface
  component in terms of a high-level, real-world goal, it is important that an Assistant not be
  the only way to execute a particular computer task.
  Often, users will need to do something on the computer that has nothing to do with a high-
  level goal: adjusting the time displayed on the on-screen clock, for example, is a simple
  operation that should not have to involve using an Assistant that is designed to support
  the goal of setting up the computer (even though setting the time is part of setting up).
  Users should be able to interact with a simple user interface component that enables them
  to adjust the time without using an Assistant.

• Integrates disparate interface elements
  Based on the identified real-world, end-user goal, an Assistant gathers the different user
  interface elements and components that support that goal. For example, an Assistant that is
  designed to help users set their Macintosh computer up for Internet access would bring
  together elements from different control panels, such as Remote Access and TCP/IP (see
  figure 3).

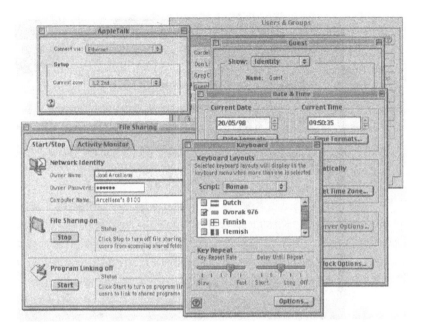

Figure 3.
Some of the user interface components that are effectively brought together in the Mac OS Setup Assistant.

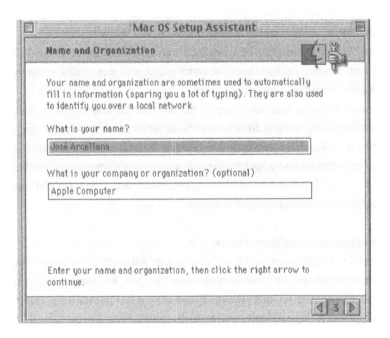

Figure 4.
The interview starts simply, with questions anyone can answer.

• Asks questions in the form of an interview, rather than giving instructions
An Assistant gets the information it needs from users by conducting an interview, asking
questions as simply as possible, explaining any terms that might need explanation within
the context of the interview, so that users do not feel the need to go outside the Assistant
for help. As a design principle, if users have to go to on-line help while using an Assistant,
then it is safe to say that the interview has faile (see figure 4).

• Makes reasonable assumptions
An Assistant's interview should be designed such that it asks only the questions it needs
answers to, asking only for that information that it is unable to extract from the user profile,
the system state, and other information it already has available. By making such
assumptions, the interview is made as short as possible, and users don't get asked what
they might consider 'stupid' questions. Again, the point of making reasonable assumptions
is to support the user goal.

5   What an Assistant is not

In contrast, an Assistant is not any of the following.

• Not a cosmetic fix for seriously flawed user interface design
In the same way that documentation should not be used to explain away badly designed
user interfaces, Assistants should not be used to cover them up. In practical terms, the
former is true and the latter will be likely; in fact, Assistant-like software is often called
upon or most appreciated when users need to confront difficult and confusing interfaces
that result as much from complex functionality as from bad design. Be that as it may,
designers should understand this principle and advance it whenever possible, as it can only
result in better interfaces and better Assistants.

• Not the only way to execute a computer task (not a utility program)
Again, it is important that an Assistant is not the only way to execute a computer tasks
because there is no way to predict all the high-level, real-world goals that users will have
that may require the execution of particular computer tasks. Further, there will be many
situations when the execution of such tasks are discrete and outside the larger context of a
high-level goal.

• Not deconstructed dialog boxes
If an Assistant is to succeed as an interaction layer between a high-level user goal and the
computer tasks that support that goal, it needs to do more than merely stagger the
presentation of the usual interfaces to those computer tasks. It should be able to do some
smart branching of the interview based on answers to previous questions, not present

elements that most users would likely leave at their default values. In general, the Assistant should make some effort to shield users from the often befuddling intricacies of dialog boxes and multi-level menus.

• Not a way to give computers a personality
Mac OS 8 Assistants are not an attempt to make the computer more 'personable' or otherwise give it human-like attributes. The tone of the language in the Assistant interview is deliberately neutral: neither effusive, nor hostile. To the extent that an Assistant has a 'personality', it would be friendly and helpful (but not solicitous), and even then the design attempts to convey that those attributes belong to the Assistant rather than the computer itself.

6   How to design an Assistant

The following sections describe the process used to design the Assistants that first shipped with Macintosh OS 8.0 system software. The process involves seven general phases, taken in sequence but not in strict, discrete order. As always, the design process involves some recursive and iterative going-back and going-over certain phases, as required by specific conditions, new information, and schedule and resource constraints. At the end of this process, you will have a design that is ready to prototype and test for usability, which in turn leads to revisions and tweaks to the design, which should be tested again for usability - and so on, schedule and resources allowing.

6.1   Know your users

The first step in designing an Assistant is to get to know, as completely as possible, the users for which it is intended. The more specific the information, the better, because the better able you are to tailor the Assistant to your specific users. The following types of information are useful in developing a profile of your users:

• How they use computers: what they use computers for, which application programs they use, in which situations and contexts they use computers; which computers they have used in the past.
• Who they are: age, gender, occupation, income, education, number of children in household, etc.
• What other products they use: fax machines, televisions, video game consoles, cellular phones, etc.

Get marketing statistics, if possible, and break down the numbers in different ways and in different segments. How many people in each age, gender, and income group, for example, are expected to attempt the goal that the Assistant supports? Work with any marketing people you have to get a sense of how your intended users break down into different segments, and then be ready to decide which user segments are significant enough that their interests outweigh the interests of other, presumably smaller user segments. In other words, try to get the marketing data that will enable you to make design decisions based on what percentage of intended users would have a better user experience and what percentage would have a worse experience based on the decision. The design principle in the case of Assistants is quite simple (and quaintly socialist): the greatest good for the greatest number. Whatever works better for more people should be the design you should choose.

6.2 Define their problem

Specify what users have to do in order to achieve their goal. Include non-computer tasks (such as using the telephone, filling out forms, etc.), and be as specific as possible. To help you be specific and to uncover any steps that may not be obvious, describe the likely scenarios in which users would attempt the goal. For example, if the goal is computer setup, find out whether your users are likely to have some kind of technical support, whether they will be in a corporate setting where a system administrator will be available, and so on.

6.3 Understand their goals in their own terms

This step is distinct from the preceding one. Problem definition is quite different from problem representation: how users understand the problem in their own minds and how they describe it to themselves. State the user goal in real-world terms, in the terms that your target users might use ('set up my computer' not 'set the values in the date and time control panel, and then set the keyboard map setting, and so on'). Stating the goal in this way to yourself is key to understanding what users really want to do and how they understand what it is they want to do.

6.4 Make reasonable assumptions

Define what you might reasonably assume about your users, about their computers, and about the context in which they will be attempting the goal that the Assistant is supposed to support. You should make these definitions both at the high level, in the way your intended users will be approaching their goal, and at the low level of each step your users will be taking in the course of accomplishing their goals. For example, if users open a program called 'Internet Setup Assistant', you could probably safely assume that they are interested in getting on the Internet (so you probably don't have to ask them that).

By asking this simple question, the Assistant can deduce much more. If users answer 'No', for example, many other questions (about IP addresses, routers, and so on) become unnecessary and therefore confusing if asked. So the Assistant does not ask those questions (see figure 5).

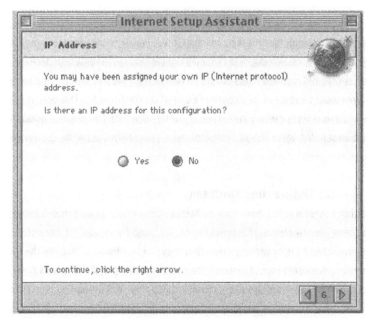

Figure 5.
It matters less that users know what an IP address is than whether or not they have one (which they can find out from a system administrator or their Internet service provider).

6.5 Ask only the necessary questions

Making reasonable assumptions becomes a process of elimination, so that you reduce to the barest minimum the information you need from your users. For example, what to name a shared folder is something that only users can decide for themselves, but even in this case you should suggest a default name for the folder (see figure 6).

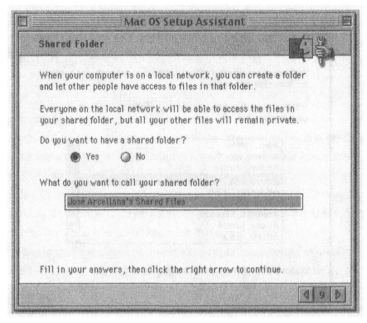

Figure 6.
If you're willing to make a bigger assumption, you may not even ask users what to name their shared folder, but in this case the Assistant plays it safe.

One question that the Assistant cannot avoid asking is where the user is located. Fortunately, this is a simple question for most users to answer, and the answer to it makes many other questions (time zone, for example) unnecessary (see figure 7).

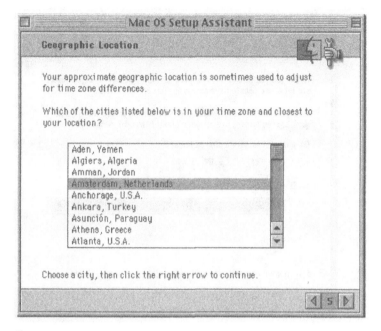

Figure 7.
Until geographic positioning systems are built into every computer (which might happen sooner than we expect), the Assistant has to ask this question.

6.6 Develop a flowchart

The penultimate step in this design process is to develop a flowchart of the interview that the Assistant conducts, showing which questions are asked, in what order, and what branches the interview takes based on the answers that users give.

Arrange your questions in a human-logical order and ask the questions in a way that makes sense to your users and is easy for them to understand. What questions would a fellow human ask of users, and in what order? For example, in a prototype version of the Assistant, it did not present the question about which version of a language the user prefers to use until after the questions regarding personal information, such as the user's name.

Of course, Macintosh system software ships in different languages, and the Assistant can determine, without asking the user, which language version of system software is running; however, certain language versions have variants. French, for example, has variants for French Canadian, Swiss French, and (just) French. Because this parameter has a bearing on keyboard maps and how keyboard input would be interpreted, it became technically preferable to ask this question ahead of the others. At the same time, the question was rephrased to suggest more the real-world analog of establishing that two people who want to converse speak the same language, so that it seemed a logical first question to users. Of course, in the real world, it is quite possible to get pretty far along in a conversation before it becomes a matter of any consequence whether one is using, say, Castillian Spanish as opposed to Caribbean Spanish.

6.7 Simplify, simplify, simplify

The final step (before prototyping and usability testing, which you should repeat as many times as resources and schedule allow) is to simplify the interview as much as possible, to look again for the opportunities where you do not have to ask for certain information, where you can explain a concept more simply or can avoid bringing up an issue that is difficult to resolve. Explain any terms you have to use that may be unfamiliar to your users, but do not start to explain subjects that are difficult to explain quickly. This approach is quite different from the terse, minimalist approach that would rather forego any explanations altogether. While often effective in documentation, a strictly minimalist approach would seem abrupt and unfriendly in an Assistant, as if it were not even trying to be helpful. Like natives dealing with a tourist who is at least trying to communicate in the local language, users appreciate an Assistant making an effort, even a token effort, to explain what may be obscure yet important. If you think of the Assistant interview as a conversation, keep in mind that you want to limit the conversation in terms of length, depth and scope, because all the Assistant really needs is certain information so that it can support the user goal. That users understand the significance and implications of that information is less important than that they correctly enter information in the interview. Specialist terminology is used in this paper, but the terminology used in Assistants, as far as possible, should be terms that the users' source of information is also likely to use so users can figure out which information they received (from their provider or administrator) is being asked for at any given point in the intervie (see figure 8).

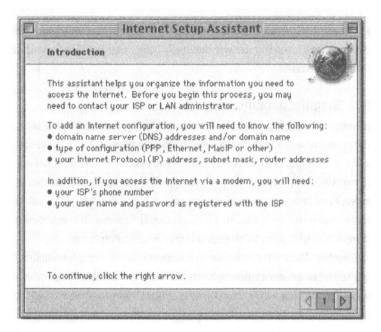

Figure 8.
When dealing with complicated information, the Assistant often has to strike a balance between
bringing up more than it can explain in a fairly simple and straightforward way and saying too little.

Remember to deliver the greatest good for the greatest number. Optimize the language and
the interaction for the majority of users, and do not complicate or compromise simplicity for
the sake of the few who will often need specialized solutions anyway.

6.8 The affective aspect

How much simplification you can effectively design into the Assistant depends mainly on
how successful you are in creating an affective atmosphere of trust and confidence. If users
assume a mindset that the Assistant will take care of everything as long as they answer
these relatively simple questions, and everything will be fine, then they will tend not to
distrust the simplifications you make. The point at which they start to wonder why the
Assistant does not say more about a 'subnet mask', for example, is the point at which you as
a designer have effectively betrayed their trust, assumed too much, and so oversimplified
the Assistant. The preferred solution in backing away from that point is not necessarily to
introduce complexity, but rather to revisit how you have gone about establishing the effect
of trustworthiness and dependability.

Establishing this affective atmosphere involves taking many steps, most of them subtle.
Taking the appropriate branch in the interview logic based on a previous answer, offering
advanced organizers and transitions into more complicated phases of the interview, using
language that is non-threatening yet not condescending, asking the right question at the

right time, and not asking the question that the computer should have the answer to - all these steps contribute to such an atmosphere and, more importantly, enable you to design a better Assistant and so create a better experience for users.

7   Future directions

Assistants in Macintosh system software are already two years old and getting more mature by the minute. In terms of the pace of this industry ('Internet time' is the unfortunate phrase), the Assistants discussed here are old and dated (though still quite effective in achieving their design goals). The obvious directions in which Assistants will probably evolve are toward a) greater apparent intelligence, with improved technologies in monitoring system states and predicting likely user intentions; b) more and bigger (but still safe) assumptions about the user, with improvements in user profiles and ways of capturing user preferences and behavior; and c) updated graphic design and introduction of richer media (such as video).

While it may seem that these considerations are primarily driven by a desire to improve the effect, the emotional content in Assistant design, to heighten the perception of trustworthiness and 'human-ness', they are in fact directed towards greater simplification for users and more effective support for larger, higher-level, more abstract goals than those that Assistants currently support.

Improvements in the affective aspect, while not incidental, will need to be tested against the perils of raising false expectations about the Assistant's actual intelligence level, for the foreseeable future. This danger, which is merely the edge of the slippery slope called anthropomorphism, could easily distract users from their real-world goals by raising new issues of trust and dependability.

References

- http://www.acm.org is a great place to start.
  See ACM's library (key words such as 'agents' or 'assistants'):
  http://www.acm.org/dl/search.html
- *Communications of the ACM* (July 1994), a special issue on Intelligent Agents:
  Maes, P., *Agents that reduce work and information overload*. Communications of the ACM
  (July 1994) and Bates, J., *The role of emotion in believable agents*. Communications of the
  ACM (July 1994). (These articles can be downloaded from: http://www.acm.org/cacm and
  http://www.acm.org/sigchi)
- Gourdol, A. and Arcellana, J., *Mac OS 8 Assistants in System 7 Applications*.
  Apple Technical Journal 27, September 1996. Sample code at:
  http://developer.apple.com/dev/techsupport/develop/issue27/arcellana.html

About the author

José Arcellana is a 'viewer/user' interface designer in Oakland, California (USA). He was at Apple Computer for more than ten years, where he worked in the areas of help and assistance, appearance, and future directions of the Macintosh human interface. In March 1999, he left Apple Computer to design World Wide Web site interfaces at NBC Internet in San Francisco.

Document and user interface design for older citizens

Herman Bouma@

Summary

The participation of older citizens in our information society is not only hampered by advancing age, but also by inadequate user interfaces. To improve this situation, the combination of the following three research factors appears to be crucial:

1. preparation of a suitable body of knowledge about the development with age of perceptual, cognitive and motor skills;
2. directed research into adaptive user interface design using agent architecture;
3. involvement of older users in the iterative evaluation of prototypes.

What is clearly lacking is a determined, concerted effort to solve these problems.

1   Older people and ICS citizenship

There are some good reasons to devote attention to interface and document design for older citizens. These people constitute a target group with special characteristics, with special needs, and operating in special environments. The basic notion is that older citizens must be allowed to participate fully in the society that they are members of. As we are well aware, our society is an information and communication society (ICS), and the user interface (UI) is the gateway to ICS citizenship. It is therefore natural that we consider this gateway to see if it indeed provides the intended access to full ICS citizenship for older citizens.

Full ICS citizenship has a number of characteristics. It provides easy access to all desired public information and to all private information. It also provides effective shielding from unwanted information, the latter being an ever present source of noise. It provides active membership of selected circles of one's own choice or profession, and, again, shielding from the many other circles outside one's interest. It supports an easy two-way private communication. Finally, it enables an easy control of one's daily environment.

As to the UI, the present situation is in crisis. Users cannot oversee the functionality, which

---

@   herman.bouma@tue.nl

is too extensive and largely hidden. Consequently, they cannot access the functionality that they want, and in navigating through the system they often lose track of where they are or how they can escape. So-called help functions seldom offer true help; often the user also gets lost in the help system which further complicates the UI. The best way to escape is to call in somebody who knows the system better, like calling in a mechanic to repair your car. But think of older people wrestling at home with their UI who make a telephone call to a help desk only to get the automated answer that they can get a certain document number by following further instructions. Indeed, going to a mechanic is easier! Also consider older people without experience of the English language because they happen to be Dutch, Spanish or Polish; what would happen to the English speaking community if they got their help information in Swedish or Chinese?

2   Demographics

In the industrial world, the proportion of older citizens is rising rather fast and this is also true for some industrializing countries. In Western Europe, the percentage of those aged 55+ is expected to rise from 20% in 1995 to 30% in 2020; for those aged 65+ the rise will be from 15% in 1995 to 20% in 2020; and for those aged 80+ from 3% in 1995 to 5% in 2020. The balance between young and old will shift towards the old. The majority of older citizens will be women. In fact, of those aged 75+, there will be twice as many women as men. Contrary to what we remember from earlier times, the great majority of the older citizens will be healthy, vital and living independently, increasingly in single-person households. This time is variously termed the 'third age', the 'golden age' or the 'silver age'. Only those 10% in the 'fourth age' will be frail and dependent on professional or family care.

It is not so easy to imagine our own society 10-20 years from now, in which older citizens will be abundant and young adults scarce. These older citizens cannot be expected to be passive. Education level and job specialization have been rising all through the 20th century, and the new generations of older citizens have learned to be both assertive and active. It is certain that they will be a very heterogeneous group, since cumulative life experiences vary so much more than amongst young adults. Generational effects will be marked in the hands-on experience with ICT, which is already the case since many older citizens (especially women) have had only limited experience with ICT in their working lives. On the other hand, the ICT dynamics in society will probably remain high for some time to come, thus keeping it difficult to catch up also for the newer generations of older citizens (Lawton, 1998). To ensure a satisfactory quality of life for older citizens, directed efforts are necessary in research, development and design (Bouma, 1992, 1998; Coleman, 1992).

3   Methodology

There exist general rules for including characteristics of users in the design process, thus providing early feedback in the prototype phase of products about usefulness and about product aspects that need improvement. Fig. 1 provides a scheme. There are a few endemic problems with such schemes. The first is that they are seldom applied according to proper methodological rules because of lack of time, money, expertise, or interest. So they tend to be replaced by easier schemes, relying on, for example, the intuition of the designer, or the specific examples of a few users in the target group that the designer happens to know, or otherwise on a non-representative sample of users. Secondly, feedback is a slow and cumbersome procedure which must be heavily supported by feed-forward knowledge. Well-established theories and knowledge about the target group should be taken into account from the very start, thus making the first prototypes already much closer to the ideal than otherwise could have been the case. However, this would imply that the knowledge needed is present within the design team, which necessitates interdisciplinary collaboration. Interestingly, for purely technical decisions, such interdisciplinary consultation seems to be the natural rule for user interfaces; however, if such consultation relates to older users it seems to be the exception. This is probably true both for interface design and document design. If a user interface is judged by its efficacy, then it is sad to note that few user interfaces fully meet their objectives. Of course, one of the aims of this conference is to raise user interface quality.

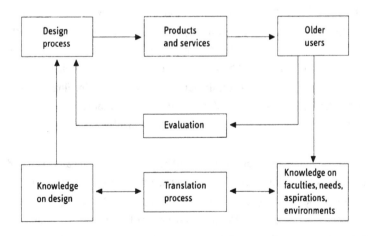

Figure 1.
Gerontechnology. How business and public bodies can create products and services suitable for elder citizens. The task of Gerontechnology is to provide insightful and fruitful connections between products/services and the older users.

4   Requirements of documents and UIs

The final test of all documents and UIs is whether or not they are effective; in other words, can they provide efficient access to the information that the user needs? Documents and UIs are generally only intermediates: the real goal of the user lies in the functionality of the information or of the system itself. So the documents about ICT systems are there to reveal functionality, to reveal access procedures, to check on normal functioning, and to offer help in the case of machine breakdown or when the user becomes lost in the system. Other types of documents may demand other types of functionality.

Good user interfaces are uniform and simple, as opposed to diverse and complex. Take remote controls as an example. In every household there are quite a few remote controls, and they all look similar. But they are hardly uniform. Each has a myriad of miniature knobs marked with small and indistinguishable icons, which indicate the possible function. Of course it is not the technical complexity that counts - take as an example the driver of a car. It does not matter to him or her if the turning of the wheels is mediated by mechanical means, by servo-motors or purely by electronic means: the only relevant function is that if he or she turns the steering wheel, the car reacts with a predictable turn. So it is the function that has to be simple and it should be obvious how to activate the function. Next it should be robust, i.e. insensitive to each kind of internal and external disturbance. Ever had a sudden blank screen or a fully unresponsive computer? Documents seem more robust though, in turn, these may be difficult to find when one needs them. The UI should also be pleasant to use, rather than duty-like, as pleasantness would seem a normal requirement in a consumer-oriented society. It should be fitting in the daily environment of use, for example in the kitchen or in the workshop or on the hobby-table. It should become adapted to its regular user by having certain adaptivities without becoming unpredictable, and it should behave as an active rather than a passive dialogue partner. Teaching should be embedded, as it is in situ that humans learn most efficiently. For domain assistance, as distinguished from UI assistance, similar requirements pertain. Finally, the design should be evaluation-driven rather than designer-driven, with representative samples of users and with proper methodology. In fact, users should be involved in the design from the very start.

This paper is about documents and UIs but both of these are means to an end and so we will briefly consider what types of end may be fitting for older users. Generally, the applications may have to do with answering concerns of the users, for example about their health, nutrition, security, and/or they may be directed at activities, hobbies or interests. Relevant application domains are the living environment (housing, daily home activities), mobility within the home and outside by foot or by private or public transport, communication with other persons, information and information gathering (navigating), entertainment, health, finances and work or hobbies.

It is said that successful aging rests on four pillars: good nutrition, daily physical exercise, frequent mental activity, and regular social contact. If we add the enabling factors and the environment, we have a full set of conditions for successful aging.

5   Faculties of older users

Most human faculties develop with age, and this is equally true for old age. We restrict the discussion to a selection of perceptual, cognitive and motor faculties. With advancing age, some of these remain rather stable whereas others show changes - usually some decline. So it is not generally true that advancing age inevitably leads to declines in all relevant aspects. Also, it should be kept in mind that there is extensive heterogeneity and that functions that decline in one person may remain stable in another. An exception to this is that, with advancing age, the rate of information processing shows some decrease and this seems to be generally true for a great many different human functions. In this paper, we will make the somewhat simplistic division between functions that are rather stable and that do not show much change with advancing age, and functions that tend to show a decline of some kind with advancing age.

The observation that a number of human functions may show a general decline with age should not be taken to mean that they are indicative of certain handicaps. A functional handicap will only present itself if the task demands cannot be met by a specific human function involved. So it is the lag between the demands of the environment and what the person needs to deal with his or her environment that determines a possible individual lag (Lawton, 1998). Any decline of function is not a linear function of age. A rule of thumb is that until the age of 75 little individual lag is present. After that, one or more such lags will gradually appear until at the age of 85 or so, individual lags tend to become dominant. Age effects in learning to use user interfaces have been studied by Docampo Rama (1997). As will be shown, the environment (including documents and user interfaces) may be designed such that the demands are lower, and consequently the lag or possible handicap is postponed.

Consequences for documents and UIs are that they should call as much as possible on stable functions while supporting or compensating for declining ones. It will not always be possible to decide beforehand what faculties are called upon and so evaluation of a representative group of older people remains a necessity. The division between perceptual or motor functions on the one hand and cognitive functions on the other is not of the either-or type; it should be kept in mind that the higher perceptual and motor functions are cognitive as well and all three are quite integrated for well known tasks. For example, reading and face recognition are higher visual faculties that depend extensively on cognitive functions and navigating uses a combination of all three.

Functional disabilities, such as low vision, blindness, hard of hearing, deafness, excessive tremor, and memory loss, usually call for specific assistive technologies. These will not be discussed in this paper.

6   Visual functions

We shall divide the visual functions into two groups: stable functions that usually do not change much with increasing age and declining functions that tend to provide increasing problems with higher age. A number of visual functions can be related to the use of documents and of UIs. Other tasks are still insufficiently understood and only indications can be given about the corresponding visual functions. If visual functions are stable, this does not mean that there are no problems connected to them. But such problems are similar for young and old alike and fall in the category of normal visual ergonomics. Even so, in cases of poor design old persons will usually experience more difficulties than young persons.

The discussion here is restricted to normal aging of visual functions (Bouwhuis, 1992; Corso, 1992) This neglects pathology. However, it should be remembered that the incidence of several eye diseases increases with age. Three prominent eye diseases of old age which cause visual decline are: cataract (decreased transparency of the eye lens), glaucoma (loss of nerve fibres) and age related macular degeneration (affecting visual cells in the centre of the retina). Nowadays, cataract operations in which the opaque eye lens is replaced by an artificial lens, are routine successes. For very high age, the division between normal and pathological aging becomes diffuse as the incidence of eye diseases gets quite high.

6.1   Stable visual functions

Good resolution of detail usually remains until advanced age, provided lighting is adequate. However, the focusing function of the eye does not. For that reason, detail vision depends on external optical correction from glasses or from corneal lenses. This usually provides for adequate detail vision at reading distance of about 30 cm and at rather long viewing distances, say beyond 3 metres. If optical correction is adequate, it also applies to other distances. So normal text of high contrast and medium size details will generally offer no reading problems for aging people. The rule of thumb is that a letter size of at least 1/200 of the reading distance is sufficient. However, many situations occur in daily life for which this minimal standard is not reached. These may involve looking at documents, computer screens and remote controls.

Colour vision generally remains stable with increasing age, except sometimes for blue. This is because of some yellowing of the eye lens that absorbs light at the shorter wavelengths. So in navigating tasks, colour guidance also remains normal, which rests on the function of colour to help one orient in the visual world and to make elements with the same colour appear related. This calls for a careful use of colours in UIs. In practice, colour is often applied for non-functional reasons, for example for visual effect. Depth vision also remains unaffected by increasing age, but plays little part in the use of documents and UIs. Higher visual functions, such as reading and face recognition, do not usually degrade, provided detail vision remains intact. Visual orientation may be less dependent on detail vision, and also offers no special problems with increasing age.

6.2 Declining visual functions

The size of the eye pupil reduces with increasing age, and absorption of light in the ocular media increases. This causes a lower illumination level of the retinal image. Since visual acuity reduces with decreasing illumination levels, detail vision by older eyes is more sensitive to illumination level. It follows that under inadequate illumination, detail vision of old people will suffer which can be overcome by a higher illumination level of the visual world. Decline of detail vision with advancing age is often due to poor illumination levels. The required individually adaptable high luminance while maintaining high contrast also applies to display screens, both of the cathode ray and liquid crystal types.

Optical focusing is a second source of decline. Focusing ability starts to decline at a very young age, but it is only at the age of 45 or so that focusing at reading distance (say 30 cm) becomes a widespread problem. As explained in the previous section, the optical correction is often such that viewing distances around 1 m are insufficient; this is a viewing distance that one often needs to read posters, read information in museums, or to recognize faces. Reading from visual displays is usually at about 50 cm, which is also not handled by normal optical correction. Varifocal spectacles or perhaps special glasses for the typical eye-display distance may help to prevent the problems.

A third decline in visual functions with advancing age concerns increased scattering of the ocular media - particularly the eye lens - which makes vision more vulnerable to glare. Glare is not restricted to road situations at night, but glare happens whenever there are bright portions of the visual field which lead to diminished contrast within the retinal image. Examples include thin lettering on a brightly-illuminated page and a computer screen in front of a daylight window. Therefore contrast on visual displays should be high and the background of the display somewhat dark. In the case of serious glare problems, it may help to reverse the image to give light lettering on a dark screen, but beyond this point a cataract operation will have to be considered.

Finally, there are changes in visual attention in the sense that rapid attention shifts within the visual field tend to be more difficult for the old than for young people (McCalley, 1995). Attention to visual objects need not be restricted to the centre of the visual field, and it is just the areas of the visual field outside the centre where the eyes are focused, that seem to be most vulnerable. Visual search is mediated by such parafoveal and peripheral vision, and what we call reading in daily life is actually often visual search: reading or viewing what one does not want to see in the search of items that one does want to see. There is recent evidence that the proper training of eye movements can partly compensate for a relative visual neglect of the peripheral visual field. Generally, much of the visual information on display screens or in documents will not be read and therefore an overload of information will be detrimental to its usefulness. Of the really useful information, proper layout and usability checks beforehand are essential, although the latter are seldom applied.

7   Hearing functions

For document and user interface design, the hearing sense is probably less relevant than vision. However, multimedia interfaces where sound plays a role are becoming more common. From the user point of view, the term 'multi-sensory' would be more adequate than the technically inspired term 'multimedia'.

Deterioration of hearing is one of the most frequent perceptual deficits of old age, and more so for men than for women. This may be due to hearing damage from too high a sound level in working life; in earlier times it was weaver's deafness and now it comes from other literally deafening sound sources. Such hearing damage will be with us for a long time, as the music scene for young people provides high sound levels which seem intended to prevent momentary speech communication, but which may result in unintended difficulties in speech communication in later life. Given the influence of high sound levels from earlier years of life, drawing a distinction between normal and pathological hearing is even more difficult than for vision.

7.1   Stable hearing functions

With increasing age, the hearing of low and medium sound frequencies up to 5 kHz is usually little affected. The frequency of 5 kHz is an important boundary since most human speech occurs in the frequency range from 0 to 5 kHz. Audible warning and alarm signals from UIs should be designed within this frequency range and preferably even somewhat on the lower side. As important as frequency composition is the signal to noise ratio (S/N ratio). The hearing of sounds with high S/N ratios is stable and usually remains so up until old age. Discrimination of sound direction is usually stable if both ears continue to have similar characteristics. It follows that single integrated sounds remain well recognizable and the same is true for well-articulated speech from a single speaker against a quiet background.

7.2   Declining hearing functions

High sound frequencies are the first to suffer with aging, and the process tends to deteriorate gradually along the sound spectrum toward the medium frequencies. Again, there are extensive individual differences. Consequently, the use of frequencies higher than 3 to 5 kHz should have no distinguishing or alarm function.

S/N ratio is a second factor to be considered. With increasing age, sounds with a lower S/N ratio become more difficult to identify. Noise here refers to all sound signals other than the speech or other signal intended to be heard. Since noise is abundant in many environments, this presents a serious problem. The first rule for proper sound communication for older people is that all unrelated sounds should be kept to a minimum. Radio and television programmes offer too many examples of such undesirable situations. Also restricting reverberation of sound by increased absorption in the listening room is worthwhile. From the above, it follows that the perceptual separation of complex mixtures of sounds may cause problems, because each sound acts as noise for another sound.

For interfaces, the S/N ratios should be kept high at all times and background sounds should be avoided. Increased S/N requirements may well mean that rapid speech suffers more from noise than slow speech; signal processing procedures are now available that automatically lower speech rate while maintaining a high speech quality. This may be expected to be very helpful.

Finally, rapid attention shifts are probably more difficult for older people to cope with in both hearing and vision. So such shifts should be kept to a minimum.

Although there are only a few ways in which hearing functions decline, actual sound environments in the present world are often detrimental to the hearing of older people. It is the auditory environment more than the declining auditory functions themselves that tend to be the cause of hearing difficulties.

8   Cognitive functions

It is perhaps the decline of cognitive functions that is feared most by aging persons and, although the incidence of dementia is age dependent, its incidence remains restricted. In this paper, we do not consider this pathological aging of cognitive functions. In fact, the term 'cognitive' refers to many types of information processing in humans. We referred earlier to reading, face recognition and speech perception, all of which are of a perceptual and cognitive nature. Reasoning processes in learning to use interactive devices have been studied by Freudenthal (1998). In this section, we will only consider memory functions. There are many types of memory and here we will only briefly indicate the most relevant types.

It is possible to define the memory functions that can be determined experimentally in such a way that some decline with age whereas other remain stable. Craik & Bosman (1992) provide an overview. This is not a self-evident procedure since there are many experimental tasks that call on more than one memory function. Consequently, the outcome will be some mixture or combination. Also, human tasks can usually be performed in more ways than just one, and so choosing a different type of solution may compensate for deficits in a particular area. In memory functions, a useful distinction is drawn between the memory content itself and the access route. The 'tip-of the-tongue' phenomenon is an example of a failing access route.

8.1 Stable cognitive functions

Primary memory can be described as the immediate recall of information. The sensory register that keeps information for periods of up to a few seconds is part of primary memory. Primary memory is rather insensitive to aging, provided that there is no interference from other information sources.

A second type of stable memory is procedural memory: the memory where well-rehearsed procedures are retained. This calls for extensive training of rather fixed UI procedures and avoidance of too many options and diversions that would disturb the well-trained pathways. So the visual layout of screens or documents should not be changed without good reason.

Thirdly, memory for earlier experienced episodes remains unaffected if schematic support is being offered.

Finally, the learning process itself is a stable function: people can and do learn at any age. However, there is no age at which people can consciously 'unlearn'. Therefore, procedures and information that have been well-learned earlier in life remain present in the background and may come to the surface at unexpected moments. Standardization and normalization are of the utmost importance for UIs and for the layout of documents.

As is well known, most learning is done in actual daily situations (situated learning); the explicit learning from books that tends to prevail in education is the less common type of learning. Recently the notion of 'generation' has been applied to technology procedures in the sense that the type of technology that one has experienced from one's early years results in very stable types of procedure. New technologies that have been encountered only later in life (with less thorough training) will cause more difficulties. The rapid advance of new technologies with novel interfaces will in itself continue to give rise to difficulties for older people. Built-in training procedures, or well designed and evaluated user instructions, can offer some help, but most help functions make the interface more complex without solving the problems of the user. With the development of a new interface architecture, a new area of research that holds promise for situated learning has recently been opened (Masthoff, 1997).

8.2 Declining cognitive functions

Working memory is a first target for aging, particularly if two tasks (the processing of information and keeping the information in memory) have to be carried out simultaneously. So it is the interference between processing and memorizing that makes such tasks vulnerable to aging. Unfortunately, combinations of tasks are often required in daily life and also in the use of documents and of interfaces. Take the simple example of looking up a telephone number for immediate dialing, or an e-mail address for retyping, and you can understand why the wrong connections are so often made. Of course, actual tasks in searching for information or in working with UIs often involve the combination of processing and memorizing. A properly designed user interface avoids this combination as far as possible, for example by taking over the memory requirements. This calls for a detailed task analysis of the user with the purpose of keeping the requirements for working memory at a minimum, by keeping the information available on the screen for immediate use.

A second type of decline is of the memory for facts or names that are insufficiently reinforced. Here, the documents and interfaces can also offer compensation by providing external memory support.

A third type of declining memory is unsupported episodic memory that has to function autonomously without either external or internal schematic support. This is relevant for episodes of procedures that for older users need external or internal schematic support. So the required schematic support should be provided externally.

The final vulnerable memory type to be mentioned is unsupported prospective memory, an internal 'alarm clock' that tells one at the proper time that a certain action has to be initiated. Such specific internal alarm functions are already difficult and open to interference from other tasks. This interference effect increases with advancing age. Clearly, such specific 'alarm-clock' functions can easily be provided by machines.

The importance of support is a common factor that can be taken into account in the design of documents and interfaces, because it is precisely such support that can be offered externally. If the support is complex, fixed procedures should prevail as supporting schemata, for example for navigation.

9   Motor functions

9.1   Stable motor functions

Although muscle force generally declines with increasing age, it can be considered as stable for document and UI purposes, since the requirements are low and can be easily met. The same is true for well-trained motor skills, if well trained implies intensive use over a long period of time. So people who have learned typing skills with the QWERTY interface at an early age, and who have kept on practicing, can be expected to remain skilled. Finally, the learning of new motor skills remains possible up at any age, although the skills will not be mastered to the same extent as when they would have been learned earlier in life.

9.2   Declining motor functions

The main factor that is affected by aging is the speed at which actions are executed, and this is true for both simple and complex motor skills. If user actions are self-paced, this does not present much of a problem, but any machine-paced actions such as any actions that have to be carried out within a certain time-window are vulnerable. So, the pace of required user actions should be low and prolongation of the allotted answer time may be useful if the first few user answers appear to come slowly.

Next, newer skills are more vulnerable than earlier well-trained skills, and there is always the possibility of unintended interference by earlier motor skills. For simple tasks, the prospects are better than for complex tasks. For example, if typing has not been learned at an early age, it becomes a rather difficult skill to master. On the other hand, learning to use the mouse for cursor moves should offer no real problems after sufficient training; the double-click is a machine-paced event and can be expected to be vulnerable; increasing the time interval for older users seems unavoidable.

Since tremor increases with age, fine motor movements will usually suffer with aging and should not be relied on in a UI designed for use by older persons.

10 Conclusion

The proportion of older people in society is quickly rising and new, different generations of older persons are emerging. The society in which they are living is rapidly changing through technological developments into an information and communication society. This makes it essential that the older people win proper control over their ICT environment since it is the only way in which they can continue to be full participants in their society. Getting access to useful ICT functions will require effort by the aging people themselves, but the main burden is on the designers of documents and interfaces to take older users seriously as consumers. Much existing insight into aging human functions can already be applied and the methodology is there to check from the very start of the design process whether the requirements are really met. What is painfully missing is a serious effort by ICT business who seem to be waiting for more consumer pressure rather than doing the proper job that society is right to expect.

References

- Bouma, H. (1992), *Gerontechnology: making technology relevant for the elderly.*
  In: H. Bouma, & J.A.M. Graafmans (eds.), Gerontechnology. Amsterdam, IOS Press, p. 1-5.
- Bouma, H. (1998), *Gerontechnology: emerging technologies and their impact on aging in society.* In: J. Graafmans, V. Taipale & N. Charness (eds.), Gerontechnology: a sustainable investment in our future. Amsterdam, IOS Press, p. 93-104.
- Bouwhuis, D.G. (1992), *Aging, perceptual and cognitive functioning and interactive equipment.* In: H. Bouma & J.A.M. Graafmans (eds.), Gerontechnology. Amsterdam, IOS Press, p. 93-112.
- Coleman, R. (1998), *Improving the quality of life for older people by design.*
  In: J. Graafmans, V. Taipale & N. Charness (eds), Gerontechnology: a sustainable investment in our future. Amsterdam, IOS Press, p. 74-83.
- Corso, J.F. (1992), *The functionality of aging sensory systems.* In: H. Bouma & J.A.M. Graafmans, (eds.), Gerontechnology. Amsterdam, IOS Press, p. 51-78.
- Craik, F.I.M. & Bosman E.A (1992), *Age-related changes in memory and learning.*
  In: H. Bouma & J.A.M. Graafmans (eds.), Gerontechnology. Amsterdam, IOS Press, p. 79-92.
- Docampo Rama M. (1997), *Age-related learning effects in working with layered interfaces.* Eindhoven, IPO Annual Progress Report 32, p. 19-26.
- Freudenthal, D. (1998), *Learning to use interactive devices: age differences in the reasoning process.* Eindhoven. PhD dissertation. Eindhoven University of Technology.
- Lawton M.P. (1998), *Future society and technology* In: J. Graafmans, V. Taipale & N. Charness (eds.), Gerontechnology: a sustainable investment in our future. Amsterdam, IOS Press, p. 12-22.
- Masthoff, J.F.M. (1997), *An agent-based instruction system.* Eindhoven. PhD dissertation. Eindhoven University of Technology.
- McCalley, L.T. (1995), *Visual selective attention and aging.* Eindhoven. PhD dissertation Eindhoven University of Technology.

About the author

Herman Bouma graduated as a visual scientist and later became director of the Institute for Perception Research (IPO). After his retirement, he continued as chairman of the Biomedical and Health Care Technology Centre and as a director of the Institute for Gerontechnology, both at the Eindhoven University of Technology. He was chairman of the scientific committee of the first international Conference on Gerontechnology in Eindhoven in 1991 and contributed an invited paper to the second Conference in Helsinki in 1996. He is a member of the Royal Netherlands Academy of Arts and Sciences.

Supportive documentation for older people

Patricia Wright[@]

Summary

We already know a great deal about how to design documentation but multimedia interfaces raise new challenges. Technological developments have many implications for the use of computers by older people. These are discussed in relation to three categories of potential problems: physical, cognitive and emotional. The interdependence of interface design and documentation requirements is illustrated.

1   Introduction

This paper has three distinct sections. The first concerns the topic of documentation itself. It is helpful to set the documentation needs of older people within the context of the evolution in the ways computer users are provided with information and the qualitative changes that have occurred in documentation because this illustrates the diversity and refinement of documentation genres. It inevitably raises questions about whether documentation, or some kinds of documents, are still needed. After establishing this context, the second section will consider the documentation implications for older people with reference to three sub-domains where age-associated impairments often occur: physical needs relating to sensory limitations, cognitive needs arising from constraints on mental resources, and emotional needs relating to personal goals. A more comprehensive account of the human factors' implications of growing older will be found in Fisk & Rogers (1997). In the final section the discussion will return to the interdependence of decisions about documentation and about the interface. This leads to a discussion of the importance of performance-based evaluation during the design process, where it will be pointed out that age is not always the most suitable variable for matching between the volunteers assisting with pilot evaluation and the target audience. Comparable knowledge, experience or interests may be more critical in some contexts.

@ WrightP1@cardiff.ac.uk

2   Why have documentation?

Most of us are able to get into an unfamiliar car and to drive it without consulting the owner's handbook. Perhaps the day may come when we are so familiar with 'driving' a range of computers that we have developed schema that enable us to know how to ask questions and get the interface to tell us about itself. It is already possible to design computer products offering rich functionality, with interfaces that are so simple they do not require documentation (Millar, 1998). I am engaged in just such a project where we are developing a memory aid on a pocket-sized computer that will be usable by people with severe memory problems. It is imperative for this audience that all necessary information for using the aid is provided on the interface itself. It is an empirical issue to see whether this style of interface is found too pedestrian and obstructive by people who do not have memory problems. Plausibly, people unfamiliar with computer products, including older people, may also find this interface supportive.

The evolution of computer documentation has introduced many changes to the ways users are provided with answers to their questions. For example online help often replaces printed reference manuals (Curtis, 1997). But online help comes in a variety of genres and the equivalent of the printed manual is often now a hypertext in which the material is subdivided into small units and readers jump around within the manual by clicking on words and phrases. Readers have discovered how to ask some questions about the interface by making gestures rather than by formulating verbal commands. For example, if there is an unfamiliar icon on the screen, it is often possible to find out what this does by moving the cursor over it and/or clicking on it. The question is then answered by a pop-up window, which some applications call a 'tool tip' and others 'balloon-help'. Many applications provide intelligent agents such as 'wizards' that give advice about procedures and shortcuts. These wizards watch what the user does and try to discern the user's goals. They then use this information to provide advice and training that will enhance performance. There is no need for users to learn about the range of procedures offered by the application, since wizards limit their advice to relevant task goals. For some functions users may be able to ask for and be given step by step advice on how to accomplish task goals. In other instances, such as preliminary tutorials, training may be provided through animated demonstrations, rather than verbal summaries of the actions to be carried out. This brief overview illustrates that documentation is not a single genre but a diverse collection of ways of answering users' questions.

What are the most helpful forms of documentation for older users? Much is already known about the features that contribute to effective document design (Horton, 1994; Schriver, 1997). It is known that the documentation needs to be context-specific so that users see only the information which is relevant to the task they are currently seeking to do. It is known that the documentation needs to be easily available, and an operational definition of this might be that help is only one mouse click away. It is known that documentation needs to be non-intrusive because documentation which forces itself unbidden upon the user tends to be very irritating. Ideally the documentation should be invoked by users and provide information in a way that can be easily followed. Increasingly it has been recognised that documents need to provide users with support for their questions, in the sense that these questions may be ambiguous in referential terms. One solution to this is the provision of an automated 'interviewer', who asks the user whether they mean this or that. All of these features of effective documents apply when designing documentation for older people. So do we need to know anything more than this? By way of illustrating why I think there is more to know, let me draw on an example of my own recent experience that illustrates the importance of considering the interdependence of the design of the interface and the design of the documentation.

I am involved in a project[1] with Nick Rogers and others, in which we are developing a very simple reminder system, evolving concepts and functionality from the work pioneered by Wilson et al. (1997) on NeuroPage. One objective of our new memory aid is to provide a diary in which patients with severe memory loss can enter the text of the reminder, the time the reminder should occur, and set an alarm to be on or off. We had worked very hard at devising a simple interface for this diary and were surprised to discover that explaining how to use it took four sides of A4 paper. Two of these pages were taken up explaining basic word processing functions and the other two covered the diary functions. As we read through these four pages we knew that this amount of detail was going to be too difficult for our patients to master. So we removed some of the functionality from the word processing system, and thereby reduced these word processing instructions from two pages to one page. Table 1 gives the flavour of how this reduction was achieved. The point being made is that focusing only on the documentation may not be the most helpful way of designing very simple, easy to use products. Changes to the interface and/or the functionality may also be necessary. So it is essential that the design of the documentation is closely coupled with decisions about the design of the interface. Documentation is not the solution to inadequate or inappropriate interface design.

1   The project on 'Helping people with memory impairments recall facts and procedures: a comparison of two computer aids for personal information management' is funded by grant PCD2/A1/215 from the National Health Service Research and Development programme for people with physical and complex disabilities, 1997-2000.

```
BEFORE
To delete a word
    Drag across word to highlight text
    Red key deletes highlighted text

To delete a letter
    Tap after the letter to be deleted to position the cursor
    When the cursor appears, press red key

To insert a letter or word
    Tap where the new text is wanted
    Use the keyboard to type the new text

AFTER
    Green arrow keys move cursor
    Keyboard inserts text

    Red key rubs out to left of cursor
```

Table 1.
Word processing revisions for memory aid.

3   Sensory needs of older people

3.1 Visual support

People with visual impairments, and this includes more than just older people, benefit not only from enhanced legibility but from the assistance afforded by consistent use of spatial cues and colour coding to add redundancy to documentation. Recent evidence shows that legibility influences not only the identification of words but also the interpretation of the meaning, especially the integration of the ideas expressed by the writer (Aberson & Bouwhuis, 1997). Furthermore this research has shown that increasing the x-height of text from approximately 5 mm to 9 mm is very helpful for people in the age range 60-80 years but that further increases in size will actually reduce the ease with which the text can be read.

Another reason why bigger is not always better is that whenever text on screen is enlarged this reduces the amount of information currently in view and so reduces the contextual cues available to aid comprehension. A compromise solution may be to provide a zoom facility, perhaps zooming sections of the text rather than the whole screen. There is also considerable evidence that older people benefit from enhanced contrast, although recent work in the Netherlands has shown that reducing blur can be even more effective in enhancing legibility (Roelofs, 1997). The use of back lighting is one of the ways in which greater contrast can be achieved on the small pocket and palm-size computers, although the brightness and greater customisability of colour screens may offer a wider range of custom solutions for an audience where visual impairments can take many forms.

In addition to the legibility of the text itself, whenever a text editing task is interrupted however briefly, there can be difficulties finding where the cursor is on the screen. Enhanced cursor identification has received relatively little attention, although some operating systems offer a few customising options and novel solutions have been proposed that involve changing the shape of the cursor and its movement characteristics (Worden et al., 1997). Additionally some simple solutions may be available. The cursor is usually the same colour as the text, whereas it would be easier to locate if it were a different colour, and many desk top and laptop computers now have colour screens.

Visual impairments reduce the discriminability of icons on the task bar and elsewhere. One way of helping users cope with this is by making use of redundant cues such as colour coding and spatial location. It may not be necessary to increase the size of the icon in order to make similar graphics more perceptually distinctive. The enhanced clarity of the graphic elements within icons, together with their meaningfulness and the ease of interpreting what the icon stands for, are features that would support most computer users, not just older people.

3.2 Auditory support

It is well-known that the elderly tend to have hearing loss but the specific pattern of this impairment differs between individuals (Willott, 1991), and so the solutions must differ too. The solution of increasing the loudness of the information provided by the interface will work for the 35% of hearing impaired people who have strial presbycusis, which is characterised by a uniform hearing loss across all frequencies (Schieber & Baldwin, 1996). However for the 12% with sensory presbycusis and the 23% with inner ear conductive presbycusis, hearing loss is greater in the higher frequencies. Consequently moving the frequency to a lower range, e.g. replacing a woman's voice with a man's voice, is more helpful than adjusting the loudness. Another form of hearing loss, neural presbycusis, selectively impairs speech perception rather than non-speech sounds. Indeed in tasks where people are listening to targets against background noise, decrements are detected for speech signals at much younger ages than for pure tone targets (Bergman, 1980). Headphones that reduce the background noise and so enhance the signal from the interface may be one solution. As infra-red links remove the need to be chained to the computer by a cable, this solution may be increasingly acceptable to users.

Older people find it particularly difficult to deal with rapid speech (Taylor et al., 1994). For people experienced in a particular task, such as older airline pilots, communication (in this case with air traffic control) can be one of the job components that is most likely to show decrements with age (Hardy & Parasuraman, 1997). Fortunately safety measures are built into this, with pilots repeating the message so that the message giver can check that it has been correctly received. Hearing loss is rarely identical for the two ears, with the result that there can be difficulty in locating the spatial source of an auditory message. Using redundancy to provide cues about source can therefore be very helpful for older people. It is also the case that when the documentation is provided across more than one modality then it assists older people if there is multi-modal redundancy. That is to say older people find it very difficult if the visual message is saying one thing while an auditory message is saying something different, even if the visual message is entirely graphic and not verbal. The two information streams need to converge if they are going to support older people and there is considerable evidence that older people find many forms of redundancy very helpful (Tun & Wingfield, 1997).

3.3 Motor support

The input controls that are currently available for computer users include touch screens, keyboard, voice, handwriting and gesture. With the help of Christine Bartram we have recently been able to compare the success rates among people aged between 57 and 68 years (average age 62 years) for input using touch screen and keyboard (Wright et al., in press). We found these people made fewer errors when using the small keyboard of the HP360 LX pocket computer than when using the Newton on-screen keyboard. This was true for all eight volunteers, irrespective of the order in which they used the two machines. To check if this was a function of something special about the Apple Newton touch screen keyboard we repeated the comparison using the US robotics Palm-Pilot. The results were very similar. The eight volunteers taking part were aged between 56-69 years (average age 62 years). One person showed no difference between the keyboards, one was more accurate with the touch-screen keyboard but six people were more accurate with the physical keyboard.

A third study using the Philips Nino showed that the error rate fell with practice but 50% of the phrases entered via the touch-screen keyboard still contained mistakes. So it appears that for older people touch-screen keyboards are not ideal for entering text. This is leading us to examine alternative input methods for our memory aid study. The possibilities include handwriting systems and voice recognition systems. However, there are individual differences within peer groups of all ages. Consequently older people will benefit from being able to select and adjust the controls and displays to suit their own pattern of impairment. This is perhaps the major conclusion to this discussion of designing documentation that supports the sensory needs of older people.

4   Cognitive needs of older people

There are scholarly tomes on the range of cognitive changes that accompany ageing (e.g. Blanchard-Fields & Hess, 1996), and there are reviews of the dynamic interdependence among cognitive processes in the context of ageing (Rabbitt, 1993). Since the present focus is on the use of documentation, this section will examine only three domains of cognitive change: memory, attention and comprehension. However, before doing this it may be helpful to address the possibility of misunderstandings arising from the structure adopted for this paper. Having started by considering the design implications of sensory constraints, this may tempt some readers to imagine that there is an underlying model of document users in which processing starts with perception followed by cognitive processes, and then culminates in an action. This is very definitely not the case. It is true that there are exceptional circumstances in which actions do result from initial perception. For example, if an alarm bell were to ring, the perceptual sensation would interrupt whatever we were doing. It would lead to a cognitive interpretation of what the noise meant and, recognising it as a fire alarm, we would evacuate the building. But this is the exception rather than the generality. In general, actions begin with cognition relating to the person's intent (Norman, 1988). This generates specific goals, together with plans for attaining those goals. It is these cognitive activities which drive the perceptual processes.

As a consequence of actions being goal oriented, people will not necessarily read information just because it is perceptually visible on the screen. If it does not seem related to their intentions they probably will ignore it. They may not even notice its presence. As a frequent computer user, but unfamiliar with the way that Word did things, it was a long time before I noticed that way down at the bottom of my large A3 screen it was giving me all sorts of helpful status information. My intent concerned the message I sought to communicate. My goals related to the word processing activities I was engaged in, my attention was focused on the lines of text. So I did not see things even though they were clearly displayed in front of me. In general, behaviour does not start with perception but with the cognitive activities relating to setting goals and planning how to attain them. Older people may differ from those younger in setting narrower, more task-related goals. They may also differ in the plans they make for attaining these goals, preferring to re-use previous plans rather than make new ones, perhaps because of difficulties evaluating the likely success of different strategies (Brigham & Pressley, 1988). This may have implications for the ease with which older people can solve problems in collaboration with others who view the problem from a slightly different perspective (Hupet et al., 1993).

Another potential miscue from the structure of this paper arises from the convenient expository simplification in dealing with cognitive processes as separate entities. Many text books also do this but it can give a false impression about the separation of different cognitive processes. In reality they intermingle and dynamically interact with each other.

To redress this, Table 2 outlines a framework which specifies some of the activities in which people engage while using computer documentation. A fuller account of this framework, which has evolved from early notions of the usability of documents (Wright, 1980), will be found in Wright (1998; 1999). It has much in common with the perspective on problem solving adopted by Van Hees (1996).

FINDING RELEVANT INFORMATION

Re-formulating the problem as one or more queries (e.g. How to unfreeze the cursor).

Setting search targets – either explicitly in a 'Find' dialogue or index listing, or implicitly when scanning through the documentation (e.g. crash, mouse, re-boot).

Skim-reading passages of the documentation in order to assess likely relevance.

INTERPRETING THE INFORMATION FOUND

Understanding the literal meaning of the text and graphics in the documentation.

Combining the meanings from the text and graphics.

Integrating the combined meaning with prior knowledge.

Drawing problem-related inferences about appropriate actions (e.g. press certain key combinations).

TAKING ACTION

From their inferences, readers generate one or more intended goals (e.g. unfreeze cursor through warm boot).

Formulating an action plan consisting of the steps for achieving the goal(s).

Often this involves deriving subgoals and correctly sequencing these.

Monitoring the outcome as each step in the action plan is carried out.

Keeping one's place in the action plan.

Deciding whether to recycle from the very beginning if the goal is not attained.

Table 2.
Summary of activities people engage in when using documentation.

From a quick glance through table 2 it will be appreciated that memory, attention and comprehension are an integral part of how people find relevant information, interpret it and act on the basis of it. They do not switch among cognitive processes successively one by one. Consequently when older people become impaired in any of these functions it can have wide ranging effects on their use of documentation. The existence of age-related decrements in performance have been well established for the domains of memory, attention and comprehension (Morrow & Leirer, 1997).

4.1 Memory

When considering the memory problems encountered by older people, it is worth remembering that these problems can arise not only from the ageing process itself but also from taking medication. Some estimates suggest that as many as two-thirds of the older population in the USA may regularly take non-prescription drugs (Hammond & Lambert, 1994). When adding those who are prescribed medication for chronic or acute illness, it is evident that the proportion of older people taking drugs is very high.

Working memory is known to decline with age (Salthouse & Babcock, 1991) and will result in older people finding it more difficult to remember any sequence of instructions they have just read. The design solution is to provide fewer steps for instructions, and to include relevant pictures or other recognition cues that can help users map between their task context and the documentation. Because recognition memory usually gives better performance than free recall, making information available on a task or icon bar will be more helpful to users wondering how to do something than having the same information hidden from view in a drop-down menu.

Memory problems impair older people when they make decisions and implement plans because such activities involve keeping track of where one is within the subgoals of the plan. Making the subgoals explicit, and sequencing them appropriately provides an external memory aid that can help users reach their goals. This may require replacing prose paragraphs with formatted lists, perhaps with numbered steps for the actions to be performed. Not only do the subgoals need to be appropriately ordered, so too do the steps for attaining those subgoals. Giving feedback, e.g. by describing the visual consequences of actions, will not only re-assure people that they are doing the right things but will help them keep track of where they are in the sequence of steps being carried out.

It is often thought that memory problems make it difficult for older people to learn new material but much of this difficulty relates to the time older people need rather than to the lower probability of attainment at the end of the learning period. For example, Charness (1989) estimated that 3 minutes of practice per year would eliminate differences in procedural skill learning. The design solution is to enable older people to learn in a self-paced environment so that they can take more time. Not only will they need more practice but, as we shall see when discussing comprehension, the practice needs to be more varied in its settings.

One of the recent discoveries when teaching patients with learning difficulties has been that errorless learning can be a very successful training procedure (Wilson et al., 1994; Wilson & Evans, 1996). If what patients did previously was correct it will be repeated and learning is enhanced; but if they made a mistake they will probably do the wrong thing again. Hence errorless learning has been found a very effective training procedure for patients with certain patterns of memory impairments. As a training technique it may also be very effective for older people but possibly for different reasons. The benefits may be related to problems of inhibition and distractibility which are known to create serious performance problems for older people (Connelly et al., 1991; McDowd & Birren, 1990). If the learning environment is tailored so that the opportunities for errors are reduced, then so too is the competition from other stimuli that may distract people from their intended next step. This point is amplified below in the discussion of our training older people to use the memory aid we are designing.

4.2 Attention

Older people seem to be more distractible than younger people (Kane et al., 1994). This is sometimes attributed to a failure of inhibitory mechanisms which enable attention to remain focused on a particular goal-related topic. The solution to problems of distractibility when designing documentation is to remove irrelevant items thereby removing the opportunities for distraction. In practice this could mean fewer simultaneous windows or fewer icons in task bars or shorter menu lists.

Older people are slower in many cognitive tasks and this includes switching attention from one topic focus to another or one modality to another (Morrow et al., 1994). Unfortunately using documentation is nearly always an embedded task, with the user primarily trying to do something else rather than wrestle with the documentation. In order to reduce the problem of attention-switching it is better to keep the documentation shallow, with information only one click away, rather than creating deep trees that involve navigation through several hierarchical nodes. This recommendation might seem to conflict with the previouscomments about training environments being free from distraction. However there may be important differences between documentation features that support the acquisition of procedures and the display features that facilitate these learned actions being performed. Similarities between the documentation and the task environment will ease the perceptual transition.

Another attentional problem faced by older people concerns fatigue. It is one of those ironic features that a group of people who need more practice, and will be slower to complete each practice episode, are also the people who become tired more quickly. Consequently practice sessions need to be kept short but they also need to be more numerous. Distributed practice is often better than a crash learning course (Baddeley, 1990) so there is nothing new in this advice. Short, distributed practice sessions may also make it easier to introduce variety into the learning contexts, which can enhance the transfer of newly acquired knowledge and skills to a wide range of novel contexts.

A very striking example of attentional failure was found by Rogers et al. (1995) in Australia. Those researchers were not working in a computer environment but were interested in the way people read medication instructions on commercially packaged medical products. To 68 people aged between 63 and 88 years they gave either a tablet box or a medicine bottle. People looked at this product and while they still had it in their hand they were asked to refer to the label and answer some questions. When asked a question for which the answer was not in view it was found that 19% of these adults failed to turn the box round, and 18% failed to rotate the bottle. Although the labels wrapped around the container, for this group of older people out of sight was out of mind. Although 80% found the information, 1 in 5 were failing to even look for information that was not immediately in view. This supports the earlier suggestion that it is preferable to have documentation visible on the screen rather than hoping that older people will seek out information hidden from view.

4.3 Comprehension

It is a convenient simplification to think of comprehension processes operating at the word, sentence and discourse levels, setting aside the dynamic interactions among these levels. Problems at the word level can exist for older people because of differences in the life styles between those employed and those who have retired. This may mean that older people are unfamiliar with terminology that is common place among younger adults. Familiarity with information technology plays a part in this. Young adults are more likely to know what a computer mouse is and why you need two cursors for many tasks. Familiarity with the technology enables people to generate synonyms and may be among the reasons why older people were found to search for information in a manual less exhaustively than younger readers (Johnson, 1990). The design solutions are to keep jargon to minimum and provide explanations of technical terms, preferably both in the text so that the writer's meaning can be understood immediately and in a separate glossary so that readers can ask questions and refresh their memory.

At the sentence level, problems arise with long sentences and syntactic complexity. Both factors increase the demands made on readers' working memory and thereby can make comprehension more difficult for older people (Wingfield et al., 1994; Wingfield & Lindfield, 1995). Keeping instructions short and simple is good advice. It is also known that older people focus on gist to a greater extent than younger people, particularly if texts are cryptic and lacking in redundancy (Tun & Wingfield, 1994). Since older people are more likely to overlook details or to forget them, any critical details within a set of instructions require additional emphasis from the document designer.

At the discourse level, older people will often have wider experience to draw on to assist in creating a mental model of the text (Noordman & Vonk, 1992), but in the absence of relevant experience they may have problems following the theme if the demands of syntactic and lexical processing increase. Whether for reasons related to the lengthening of the processing time or to limits on cognitive resources, the need to devote more cognitive effort to lower-level processing detracts from the higher level representation of the text.

Discourse comprehension involves inference processes. For older people the inferences drawn when reading may be narrower than those drawn by younger people and the mental model being built is changed less as more information becomes available (Hamm & Hasher, 1992). For documentation the design solution is to make the inferences explicit. The value of this for people reading non-computer instructions has been demonstrated by Frantz (1994) who found that when the instruction on a paint varnish container said 'Use in a well-ventilated area' only 20% of a group of 20 adults opened the window. Making the need to open the window explicit resulted in 80% compliance from another group. Frantz found a similar pattern with the implicit instruction, 'Avoid contact with eyes' compared with the explicit instruction 'Wear goggles while applying sealant'. So documentation needs to relate general principles to a variety of contexts in which they apply. This will help older people to generalise and broaden the inferences they make.

In computer documentation an important feature of the discourse structure is the relation between verbal text and accompanying graphics. Processing verbal material is cognitively demanding, so the addition of illustrations or demonstrations is particularly helpful (Morrell & Echt, 1997). In a recent study conducted in collaboration with Professor Patrick Rabbitt and Jeanette Garwood of the Age and Cognitive Performance Centre at the University of Manchester, UK, we contrasted the performance of younger and older people on instructions for operating unfamiliar appliances. The operations consisted of clicking screen items in a particular sequence. We contrasted two ways of giving these instructions. They were either shown as verbal text on screen or were non-verbal and a visual pointer indicated the item to be clicked. For both kinds of instructions people responded by clicking the appropriate item, thereby establishing that they understood what they had to do. When starting this study we thought of this walk-through procedure as a control condition showing that both the verbal and the non-verbal instructions could be correctly interpreted. However we found that people adopted different strategies with these two kinds of instructions, especially different re-reading strategies. When people walked through the sequence of steps for a particular appliance, they could choose either to carry out the operations from memory or to repeat the sequence of instructions. They could go through the instructional sequence as often as they wished, and if they forgot what to do next when working on their own they could re-visit the instructions. We found that with verbal instructions older people took more time before going solo themselves than when the instructions were non-verbal. For younger people there was little difference between verbal and non-verbal instructions; as expected they were much faster with both than the older people.

This difference between verbal and non-verbal instructions for older people may result from problems in understanding or remembering verbal material, or it may reflect older people's confidence in their understanding or memory of those instructions. We are planning to distinguish between these possibilities but the documentation solution may be to combine both forms of instruction, perhaps moving the verbal from the visual to the auditory modality. Since information overload is a problem that older people have along with the rest of us, the use of converging information and redundancy within documentation benefits both them and us.

5   Emotional support for older people

Older people may have greater anxiety in approaching new tasks and new environments than do younger people. Design solutions include learning environments such as those pioneered by Jack Carroll with his notion of 'training wheels' (Catrambone & Carroll, 1987; Carroll, 1990). Older people also tend to become more field-dependent, that is to say they rely more on cues in the surrounding environment (Lachman, 1986, 1991). The documentation implications of this are that they benefit from highly structured material and from feedback throughout the task. There is some evidence that for older people the locus of control moves outward from the individual. Teenagers believe they can change the world; older people realise that others have a say in this and chance also plays a part. Perhaps it becomes a vicious circle that people's perception of their own declining cognitive abilities results in them seeking more help and so accepting less control over their own lives (Grover & Hertzog, 1991). Documentation may need to reassure older people that it is safe and appropriate for them to be in charge of the interaction. Fierce dialog boxes admonishing users for incorrect actions can undermine the confidence that was being built, whereas putting helpful advice in the dialog boxes can be quite successful (Grayling, 1996). The design of the documentation cannot be considered in isolation from the design of the interface and the style of the interaction as a whole.

One way of helping older people regain a sense of control is to provide advanced organisers within the documentation because these offer users a schema for what is coming up so that they are prepared for the information. Older people tend to be much more cautious than younger people, which in some tasks results in greater accuracy because they set the speed-accuracy trade-off differently from younger people (Salthouse, 1984). This may have implications for their curiosity. In our work with older people using a memory aid, the computer had a keyboard with many additional function keys. Some of these keys are brightly-coloured - a green key with a light bulb icon, the Microsoft Windows logo. Twenty older people have used the machine but nobody has asked about any of the keys on the keyboard that we had not explained to them. This behaviour is not specific to interaction with computers. From studies in the domain of healthcare information there is evidence that older people are less likely to seek out additional information when told they have a serious illness (Meyer, Russo & Talbot, 1995). Training methods that rely on exploratory learning would seem inappropriate for older people.

There may be many reasons why older people curtail their curiosity. They may fear that if they ask questions they will not understand the answer. They may be concerned that they are already having to remember a lot of new things and they do not want to burden themselves unnecessarily. Such reluctance may be off-set by pointing out the task relevance, providing realistic goals and giving the assurance of feedback en route to attaining those goals. Older people are not reluctant to tackle information technology but they may not have a vision of how it could help them. For example, after people had used the memory aid we asked them if their attitude had changed towards computers.

One person replied: "Oh yes. I never realised they could actually be useful before."

6   Interdependence of Interface Design and Document Design

In order to support inexperienced users it is possible to devise interaction styles that are slower but safer. These constrain the users' options and provide prompts to guide the interaction. They do not necessarily remove any of the functionality, they may simply change the way this is accessed. The following example comes from our work with the memory aid being devised by Nick Rogers. He developed a three function diary that enabled text to be entered, times to be specified and alarms to be activated. He also developed a version of this diary where only one function at a time was ever active. Both diaries offered the same functions and required the same actions, but they differed in the constraints on what users could do at any one time and also in the support they offered users. In the unconstrained version the three functions filled the available space in the small window, whereas when only one function was available the documentation accompanying this function could be shown on the screen. Our preliminary data collection with this interface suggests that older people find it very easy to use, their confidence grows and they easily make the transition to the three-function interface.

Variety might be the spice of life but older people may be less flexible in their choice of strategy, and once having found a successful strategy may prefer to stick with it. One design implication of this is they want fewer options. For examples word processors allow text to be deleted in several ways, but one way may suffice for older users. People will vary in how soon they feel comfortable moving from the more to the less constrained environments. So it helps if both the interface and the documentation can be customised - although of course documentation may be needed to explain how to achieve customisation.

Another facet of the interdependence of the interface and the documentation concerns the psychology of asking for help. Not everyone recognises their need for help. Many of us know that we have persevered with certain ways of doing things because they were familiar, rather than turning to the documentation in order to find a quicker way for a specific task. After the need for help has been recognised people need to know how to get it. Reading the manual or telephoning the help centre are among the options. Recently document design experts, who had given a great deal of thought to their new online help system, found that in practice it was used less often than they had hoped; they commented that the help desk seemed to provide a reading service for people reluctant to read online help for themselves (Grayling, 1998). Making salient the sources of extra information may help reluctant searchers.

People may recognise the need for help and know how to ask, but for various reasons may not be willing to ask. One of the reasons for unwillingness is that people may need to know quite a lot in order to be able to ask the right question (Miyake & Norman, 1979). It can be all too easy to miscommunicate with an online help system. I remember the half hour wasted when, as an unfamiliar user of Microsoft Word, I had created some text and wanted to put a frame around it. Within the online help it was easy to locate information about the frame command but it only told me the steps to carry out. Whenever I printed the page there was no frame to be seen. Eventually I discovered that what I called 'frame' the software package called 'border'. As a new user, I did not know enough to ask the right question. Inevitably this has consequences for users' willingness to turn to the help system on subsequent occasions.

No matter how much we may discover about the factors that can make documentation easier to use, it will remain the case that user-testing is essential. The limited screen size of computer monitors means that there will always be trade-offs that designers have to make in a context-specific way. Certainly the development of our memory-aid benefited from the user-testing we carried out. For example, we imagined that when people were using the stylus as a pointing device for the touch screen that it would be of no consequence whether they were right-handed or left-handed. After watching our first left-handed volunteer wrestle with the stylus and the screen when making diary entries and setting times we realised how mistaken we had been, although data collected by Darren Walker at the University of Exeter, UK, shows that the use of a touch-screen keyboard is no poorer for left-handers.

When conducting user tests it is not necessarily the case that age is the most important characteristic on which people should be matched. Peers of any age can vary widely in their cognitive abilities and this remains the case for older people (Rabbitt, 1990). Let me illustrate this point with a hypothetical scenario. Imagine that Arnold, a 62 year old man with plenty of financial support, wanted an interface and appropriate documentation for a bespoke application. Arnold is a statistician and uses computers in his work.

He is someone who likes opera and he is divorced. Consider the following pen-pictures of two potential volunteers for pilot testing and decide which would be the most appropriate person for getting useful feedback about the new interface. One of the potential volunteers is Colin who is also male and 62 years old. He left school at 14 and is now a very successful landscape gardener. He lives in the country, likes fishing, is married and has horses and dogs. His children, who are now adults, were teenagers before having computers in the home was popular. The other available volunteer is very different. Her name is Barbara and she is 24 years old. She has a masters degree in Business Administration and works with financial planning software, using computers daily in her work. She too is a town dweller and likes concerts. (The significance of an interest in music is that she is likely to have equipment in the home that needs setting and adjusting.) She is unmarried. The choice between piloting the interface with someone having the same gender and age as Arnold or someone who has similar knowledge, background and interests, highlights that age may not be the most important matching variable.

7   Conclusions

Documentation, in the broadest sense of the design of both interface and ancillary advice, is improving. Advances in technology are meeting older people's needs arising from sensory impairments. In addition we are learning how to structure tasks and to design interfaces that will reduce the demands on people's cognitive resources. We are just beginning to recognise the importance of emotional factors as determinants of people's ability to use computer-based products successfully. As we improve computer use for older people, the design of the interface and the documentation improves for us all. Enabling users to customise the interface to suit their own preferences and specific purposes is a design feature that supports a far wider group than just older people.

References

- Aberson, D.H. & Bouwhuis D.G. (1997), *Silent reading as determined by age and visual acuity.* Journal of research in reading 20, p. 184-204.
- Baddeley, A.D. (1990), *Human memory: theory and practice.* Sussex, Lawrence Erlbaum Associates.
- Bergman, M. (1980), *Aging and the perception of speech.* Baltimore, University Park Press.
- Blanchard-Fields, F. & Hess, T.M. (1996), *Perspectives on cognitive change in adulthood and aging.* New York, McGraw-Hill Companies.
- Brigham, M.C. & Pressley, M. (1988), *Cognitive monitoring and strategy choice in younger and older adults.* Psychology and aging 3, p. 249-257.
- Carroll, J.M. (1990), *The Nurnberg funnel: designing minimalist instruction for practical computer skill.* Cambridge, MIT Press.
- Catrambone, R. & Carroll, J.M. (1987), *Learning a word processing system with guided exploration and training wheels.* In: J.M. Carroll & P.P. Tanner (eds.), Proceedings of CHI+GI87: Human factors in computing systems and graphics interface. New York, ACM Press, p. 169-174.
- Charness, N. (1989), *Age and expertise: responding to Talland's challenge.* In: L. Poon, D.C. Rubin, & B.A. Wilson (eds.), Everyday cognition in adulthood and late life. New York, Cambridge University Press, p. 437-456.
- Connelly, S.L., Hasher, L. & Zacks, R.T. (1991), Age and reading: the impact of distraction. *Psychology and aging* 4, p. 533-541.
- Curtis, J. (1997), *Managing hardcopy documentation in a multiplatform environment.* In: Crossroads in communication. Proceedings of 15th annual international conference on computer documentation. New York, ACM Press, p. 35-37.
- Fisk, A.D. & Rogers W.A. (1997), *Handbook of human factors and the older adult.* San Diego, Academic Press.
- Frantz, J.P. (1994), *Effect of location and procedural expliciteness on user processing of and compliance with product warnings.* Human factors 36, p. 532-546.
- Grayling, T. (1998), *Fear and loathing of the help menu: a usability test of online help.* Technical communication 45, p. 168-179.
- Grover, D.R. & Hertzog, C. (1991), *Relationships between intellectual control beliefs and psychometric intelligence in adulthood.* Journal of gerontology: psychological sciences 46, p. 109-115.
- Hammond, S.L. & Lambert B.L. (1994), *Communicating about medications: directions for research.* Health communication 6, p. 247-252.
- Hamm, V.P. & Hasher L. (1992), *Age and the availability of inferences.* Psychology and aging 7, p. 56-64.
- Hardy, D.J. & Parasuraman, R. (1997), *Cognition and flight performance in older pilots.* Journal of experimental psychology: Applied 3, p. 313-348.

- Hees, M.M.W. van (1996), *User instructions for the elderly: what the literature tells us.* Journal of technical writing and communication 26, p. 521-536.
- Horton, W. (1994), *Designing and writing online documentation: hypermedia for self-supporting products.* New York, John Wiley & Sons.
- Hupet, M., Chantraine, Y. & Neff, F. (1993), *References in conversation between young and old normal adults.* Psychology and aging 8, p. 339-346.
- Johnson, M.M. (1990), *Age differences in decision making: a process methodology for examining strategic information processing.* Journal of gerontology: psychological sciences 45, p. 75-78.
- Kane, M.J., Hasher, L., Stoltzfus, E.R., Zacks, R.T. & Connelly, S.L. (1994), Inhibitory attentional mechanisms and aging. Psychology and aging 9, p. 103-112.
- Lachman, M.E. (1986), *Locus of control in aging research: a case for multi-dimensional and domain-specific assessment.* Psychology and aging, 1, p. 34-40.
- Lachman, M.E. (1991), *Perceived control over memory aging: developmental and intervention perspectives.* Journal of social issues, 47, p. 159-175.
- McDowd, J.M. & Birren, J.E. (1990), *Aging and attentional processes.* In: J.E. Birrren & K.W. Schaie (eds.), Handbook of the psychology of aging. San Diego, Academic Press, p. 222-230.
- Meyer, B.J.F., Russo, C. & Talbot, A. (1995), *Discourse comprehension and problem solving: decisions about the treatment of breast cancer by women across the life-span.* Psychology and aging 10, p. 84-103.
- Millar, C. (1998), Making manuals obsolete: getting information out of the manual and into the product. *Technical communication* 45, p. 161-167.
- Miyake, N. & Norman, D.A. (1979), *To ask a question, one must know enough to know what is not known.* Journal of verbal learning and verbal behaviour 18, p. 357-364.
- Morrell, R.W. & Echt, K.V. (1997), *Designing written instructions for older adults: learning to use computers.* In: A.D. Fisk & W.A. Rogers (eds.), Handbook of human factors and the older adult. San Diego, Academic Press. p. 355-361.
- Morrow, D. & Leirer, V.O. (1997), *Aging, pilot performance and expertise.* In: A.D. Fisk & W.A. Rogers (eds.), Handbook of human factors and the older adult. San Diego, Academic Press, p. 199-230.
- Morrow, D., Rodvold, M., McGann, A. & Mackintosh, M.A. (1994), *Collaborative strategies in air-ground communication.* In: Proceedings of the Aerotech '94 conference, paper 942138.
- Noordman, L.G.M. & Vonk, W. (1992), *Readers' knowledge and control of inferences in reading.* Language and cognitive processes 7, p. 373-391.
- Norman, D.A. (1988), *The psychology of everyday things.* New York, Basic Books.
- Rabbitt, P.M.A. (1990), *Applied cognitive gerontology: some problems, methodologies and data.* Applied cognitive psychology 4, p. 225-246.
- Rabbitt, P.M.A. (1993), *Does it all go together when it goes?* Quarterly journal of experimental psychology 46A, p. 385-434.

- Roelofs, A.A.J., (1997), *Image enhancement for low vision*. PhD dissertation, Eindhoven University of Technology.
- Rogers, D., Shulman, A., Sless, D. & Beach, R. (1995), *Designing better medicine labels*. Report from the Communication Research Institute of Australia.
- Salthouse, T.A. (1984), *Effects of age and skill in typing*. Journal of experimental psychology: General 13, p. 345-371.
- Salthouse, T.A. & Babcock, R.L. (1991), *Decomposing adult age differences in working memory*. Developmental psychology 27, p. 763-776.
- Schieber, F. & Baldwin, C.L. (1996), *Vision, audition, and aging research*. In: F. Blanchard-Fields & T. Hess (eds.), Perspectives on cognitive change in adulthood and aging. New York, McGraw Hill, p. 122-162.
- Schriver, K.A. (1997), *Dynamics in document design*. New York, John Wiley & Sons.
- Taylor, J., Yesavage, J., Morrow, D., Dolhert, N. & Poon, L. (1994), *Effects of information load and speech rate on young and older aircraft pilots' ability to read back and execute air traffic control instructions*. Journal of gerontology: Psychological sciences 49, p. 191-200.
- Tun, P.A. & Wingfield, A. (1994), *Speech recall under heavy load conditions: age, predictability, and limits on dual task interference*. Aging and cognition 1, p. 29-44.
- Tun, P.A. & Wingfield, A. (1997), *Language and communication: fundamentals of speech communication and language processing in old age*. In: A.D. Fisk & W.A. Rogers (eds.), Handbook of human factors and the older adult. San Diego, Academic Press, p. 125-149.
- Willott, J. (1991), *Aging and the auditory system*. San Diego, Singular Publishing Company.
- Wilson, B.A., Baddeley, A.D., Evans, J.J. & Shiel, A. (1994), *Errorless learning in the rehabilitation of memory impaired people*. Neuropsychological rehabilitation 4, p. 307-326.
- Wilson, B.A. & Evans, J.J. (1996), *Error free learning in the rehabilitation of individuals with memory impairments*. Journal of head trauma rehabilitation 11, p. 54-64.
- Wilson, B.A., Evans, J.J., Emslie, H. & Malinek, V. (1997), *Evaluation of NeuroPage: a new memory aid*. Journal of neurology, neurosurgery, and psychiatr 63, p. 113-115.
- Wingfield, A., Alexander, A.H. & Cavigelli, S. (1994), *Does memory constrain the utilisation of top-down information in spoken word recognition? Evidence from normal aging*. Language and speech 37, p. 221-235.
- Wingfield, A. & Lindfield, K.C. (1995), *Multiple memory systems in the processing of speech: evidence from aging*. Experimental aging research 21, p. 101-121.
- Worden, A., Walker, N., Bharat, K. & Hudson, S. (1997), *Making computers easier for older adults to use: area cursors and sticky icons*. In: S. Pemberton (ed.), Proceedings of CHI97: Human factors in computing systems. New York, ACM Press, p. 266-271.
- Wright, P. (1980), *Usability: the criterion for designing written information*. In: P.A. Kolers, M.E. Wrolstad & H. Bouma (eds.), Processing visible language, 2. New York, Plenum Press, p. 183-205.

- Wright, P. (1998), *Printed instructions: can research make a difference?*
  In: H. Zwaga, T. Boersema & H. Hoonout (eds.), Visual information for everyday use: design
  and research perspectives. London, Taylor & Francis.
- Wright, P. (1999) *Designing healthcare advice for the public.* In: F. Durso (ed.) Handbook of
  applied cognition. Chichester, John Wiley & Sons, p. 695-723.
- Wright, P., Bartram C., Rogers, N., Emslie, H., Evans, J., Wilson, B. & Belt S. (in press), *Text
  entry on hand-held computers by older users.* Ergonomics.

About the author

Professor *Patricia Wright* was a senior scientist at the Medical Research Council's Applied
Psychology Unit in Cambridge, England, where she explored many aspects of information
design relating to the use of functional texts. Following the demise of APU, she has moved
this research - which is still funded by the Medical Research Council - to Cardiff University
in Wales where it focuses on the design of medical and healthcare information in print and
electronic media. Another current project, funded by the NHS R&D, explores how
information design can support ailing cognitive performance, e.g. through palmtop memory
aids.

Document-supported communication: design of new forms of interaction

Dominic Bouwhuis[@]

SUMMARY

Documents came about as a result of the perceived weaknesses of spoken communication. A systematic analysis of human communication processes reveals not only that these are in principle uncertain, but also where support could be provided that reduces this uncertainty. Despite being a repository of reliable and accurate information, advanced documents can attain a high degree of interactivity. Yet, even though they will not supplant the partners in a dialogue, their ultimate value is critically dependent on functioning as partners.

1   Introduction

In the late 1980s one of the many *Esprit*[1] research projects focussed on the development of the paperless office. It was reasoned, not entirely without logic, that the powerful way in which digital documents could be produced, handled and distributed would in time eliminate the need for paper documents altogether. At the same time, all the disadvantages of paper, (for example, storage and retrieval) would disappear, which would greatly improve efficiency. Essentially the only thing needed for this, beside the standard digital equipment, was a scanner to transform all printed text into digitally stored text. Now, some twelve years later, the best place to buy paper of any kind is the computer store. Its best selling product is the printer. The acronym *Wysiwyg*[2] reflects the fact that all text processors have printed output as their main purpose. The ubiquitous copier only serves to multiply the number of paper documents with identical copies. From a digital point of view this seems not only wasteful, but also a needless encumbrance. While the advent of electronic mail suggests that the physical distribution of paper documents by mail might have been reduced, this turns out to be wrong. On the contrary, postal services have observed that electronic mail has caused an increase in the streams of physical mail, as in many cases text and messages need to be sent as confirmation after e-mail exchange. Nevertheless, the proponents of the

[@]   d.g.bouwhuis@tue.nl
1   ESPRIT: European Strategic Programme for Research and Development in Information Technology.
2   WYSIWYG is the acronym of 'What You See Is What You Get', meaning that the screen representation of the document matches exactly the version to be printed.

paperless office were not all wrong; modern offices employ digital documents on a very large scale, and probably do even more with them than could have been anticipated in the late eighties.

As it is, writing on paper is one of the most powerful and productive developments in the history of human civilization. This was even strengthened by the first three very influential direct manipulation computer programs: MacDraw, MacPaint and MacWrite. The only thing they did was to produce a graphic illustration, a text, or both and send it to a printer to be output as a document. The tools used in these programs referred explicitly to physical graphic tools: a brush, a pencil, a spray painter, a tin of paint, an eraser. Of course, the keyboard remained the closest possible copy of the typewriter keyboard. These programs were the model for all subsequent programs that are now the mainstay of commercial computer programs. Certainly the times have changed them; they have become slower, they use far more memory, they crash more often, and one has to take courses to work with them, but basically they are the same as the first ones and they all ultimately produce printed paper. There must be something about printed paper that satisfies a need that seems to be universal and shows no sign of abating. Indeed, we see signs appearing on letter boxes saying: 'no junk mail'. Production of print is at an all time high. There must be several reasons for this state of affairs, and indeed there are; they are closely connected to our human perceptual and cognitive faculties; to social needs and to our motoric and physical properties. The heavy use of printed documents makes them seem common and unexciting; yet their commonness hides their perfect match with human use and needs.

2   History

Documents originated with the development of writing. Writing came into being by a need that was far removed from any linguistic or literary considerations; it was necessitated by purely commercial needs, not social needs, nor even religious ones. Religion made predominantly use of sculpture: a direct representation. The Bible, therefore is comparatively late, and definitely not the origin of script.

Trade requires the transport of objects, animals and commodities from the current to the next owner. How can you be sure that the stock arriving at the buyer was the same as that was sent by the seller? Clearly, some form of representation was needed beyond the stock itself. Essentially, this is the major step towards symbolic representation, just as verbal language is. But verbal language had existed for hundreds of centuries already. Until the advent of writing, language had only sculpture as its artefactual associate, not very old itself, with the first objects dating from about 40,000 BC (Valladas, et al., 1988). But then, from about 10,000 BC, in the area of Sumeria, nowadays Iran and Iraq, items of stock were represented as tokens made of clay (see figure 1).

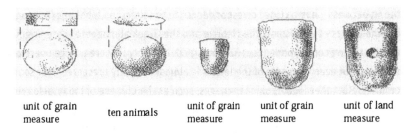

| unit of grain measure | ten animals | unit of grain measure | unit of grain measure | unit of land measure |

Figure 1.
Items of stock represented as tokens made of clay.

A small sphere could represent 5 sheep, a triangle a bushel of grain, and a ring 4 amphora's of wine. (Schmandt-Besserat, 1981). In order to keep these tokens together during dispatch, they were sealed in an envelope, also made of clay (see figure 1). Later, traders realized that it was not necessary to send all tokens, but that it was sufficient to impress them in the clay envelope, and just send the envelope which bore the impressions (see figure 2).

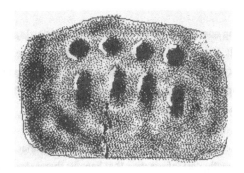

Figure 2.
A clay envelope with impressions.

Thus, the envelope became a kind of waybill, or bill of lading; it no longer contained anything, but could be read. It symbolized goods, but also required one step of abstraction to associate the symbols in a one-to-one fashion with the goods. The impressions themselves acquired a more abstract character over time. Note that the objects representing the goods were already symbolic, so that the impressions were not pictographic but logographic; they stood for a concept. In due course the impressions were rendered with a set of cuneiform signs impressed by a stylus in clay. In any logographic script the ambiguity is high, and this is why some five thousand years ago the logograms were supplemented by signs of a phonetic nature, indicating how they should be pronounced (Coe, 1992).
A logogram usually stands for a single morpheme, and the sounds of the morpheme - especially

the initial ones - have a close correspondence to the letters in alphabetic languages. Tracing back the letters of the Roman, the Hebrew and the Greek alphabet to these origins, still reveals striking correspondences (Gordon, 1962). Not only is there a large overlap in letter identities, but even the order of the letters is almost perfectly preserved over so many centuries. But other logographic languages, such as the Chinese of today, also rely heavily on phonetic characters added to the signs. There is no important script today that is not highly phonetic, even if at the same time they have a strong semantic component, for example Chinese (Coe, 1992). So, in stark contrast to what Gelb (1952) asserted about the early writing systems and the current alphabetic script, phonetic content was already a basic property in the earliest writing systems. This means that successful scripts must be closely related to spoken language - the most direct means of communication between people. Conversely, this means that words, the words that we speak and write, have an immediate meaning for us, the accessibility of which may be diminished by more abstract systems, and paradoxically, also by more pictorial systems. The fashionable trend towards pictures in preference to text in documents, (supposedly to provide more clarity and immediate meaning), seems, therefore, at best questionable. The picture trend may have more to do with the greater ease with which pictures can be produced rather than with a well-established perceptual fact.

Considering all this, the interesting question is why a document, such as a clay tablet, was deemed necessary at all. All goods, transferred between seller and buyer have a transporter, who, in principle, could communicate the details of the transport orally. The apparent fact that this was not considered sufficient suggests that the principal function of the document was 'proof', providing evidence that can be trusted: a kind of guarantee.

For several reasons, human beings cannot always be trusted; they may have other interests than their trading partners, and, consequently, give information that benefits themselves, rather than the recipients of the information. Also, human beings are fallible; they forget things, they may make mistakes, or they may speak a different language. Also, spoken language is essentially fleeting information; it leaves no trace when it has been pronounced. Ideally, then, the carrier of the information should not be self-interested and be inherently stable. For this purpose the need for a physical representation is self-evident; it is impersonal and a form can be chosen that preserves the information for as long as is desired. In the case of impressions in clay, the clay is left to harden, and this will be completely satisfactory in the arid environment in which the tablets were used[3].

---

3   After immersion in water, the impressions could be removed easily and replaced by other symbols for reuse. Though the impressions could be made permanent by simply firing the tablets, this was very rare and usually happened only accidentally in cases of fire.

3 Trust

The idea of a physical, durable representation of information therefore seems to a large degree motivated by the need for reliability. Reliability means that a communicated state of affairs can be trusted. Trust is important in environments that are subject to uncertainty, hazards and insecurity. A physical representation also implies an extent of temporal continuity, that is, it can be used as a memory. As mentioned earlier, speech does not serve as memory, and so script in the form of a document was the first means to express arbitrary issues in a more or less permanent form. As such, a document is a considerable extension to the human faculties, that had so far relied on speech and memory of spoken information. It is important to realize that it is not just the fact that something can be represented in physical form that makes it sufficient to be used as a token of trust, or as memory. It is the abstract nature of the symbols that allows the full expression of which natural language is capable, and that makes it truly useful and efficient, unlike sculpture, drawing or painting. The powerful nature of the written document persists on to this day. Diplomas, licenses, agreements, contracts, passports; an endless range of forms in the civil service, trade and commerce are written, or rather printed forms, and it is hard to imagine that any alternative proof of validity of the information contained therein would be accepted. Money is an interesting example. Metal coins are still somewhat similar to the embossed clay tablets, but paper bills seem the ultimate examples of tokens of trust. In most countries the central bank promises to pay the bearer of the banknote the sum of money printed on it. It is supposed to be the silver, or the gold represented by it. Of course, nobody ever asks for it, and banks will never do such reckless things. The existence of banknotes, therefore, relies purely on mutual trust, which is mediated by a printed document. The importance of this was made clear some years ago in Russia, when the value of the rouble rose unexpectedly. It turned out that this was entirely due to a paper shortage, preventing new banknotes from being printed and so causing paper money to be in short supply. Of course, there was hardly a connection between the actual amount of money and the amount of banknotes, and so this seems a novel and also logical idea to fight inflation. Permanence has one other feature that sets it apart from digital representation. The physical substrate of the information should be unchangeable, at the risk of losing its validity. Things that can be changed by untraceable tools, that can be copied indefinitely, that can be manipulated into whatever form, have lost their character of permanence, of validity of representation. Current computer software and hardware reinforce this view. This is a reason why the printed document will easily survive current digital representation techniques.

When considering new forms of documents, it is useful to remember that the two essential aspects - permanence and reliability - remain basic requirements for the function of documents. These are not requirements that are likely to diminish. Yet, there are other properties that give written and printed documents their unique usability. These will be discussed first before moving on to the advantages of digital documents.

4   Production

A frequently underestimated factor in the usability of human tools is miniaturization.
Representing an object by a symbol obviates the need for handling the object itself and its
bulk, and this can be seen as one way to minimize spatial extent. Manipulating symbols is
in most cases incomparably easier than manipulating the objects themselves. However, this
is not enough. Symbols must also be easy to construct, and certainly not more difficult than
it is to produce the object in question. When tokens representing objects were embossed in
clay, they still bore some resemblance to the objects, so the tokens would have to be stored
for reuse. Storage was eliminated by making the object impressions not any more with
tokens, but with impressions of a wedge-shaped stylus, which produced so-called
cuneiform characters. The original token impressions were imitated by a number of stylus
impressions, but the latter soon changed to patterns that were easier to produce. The
interesting issue here is essentially ease of production. The only things one needed to
produce a meaningful document was a clay tablet and a stylus.

When minimal tools are needed for writing, the next question is how fast writing can be
produced. To attain a high writing speed, those body parts should be used that have the
highest movement frequency, which happen to be the finger tips moving at approximately at
eight Hz. Since letters have an internal structure, the maximum number of letters to be
produced in a second is about 4, leading to some 40-60 words per minute; a very realistic
number. No body part can make faster coordinated sustained movements. However, in
connection with the mass-spring characteristics of the articulated system of the hand, the
size of the phalanges largely determines the amplitude, which is, (not surprisingly), the size
of letters. It is less surprising then that different handwriting techniques all lead to a similar
size and speed. There is a large number of alphabetic writing systems that all show the
same letter size. A syllabic script has more characters than alphabetic scripts and so the
characters are more complex. Altogether this results in the same character size and the
same writing speed in terms of number of words per unit time. Remarkably, Powell (1982)
found out, by training himself on cuneiform writing with a stylus on clay, that he attained a
writing speed similar to that of normal writing with a pen.

So, it is understandable that letters are not larger. Writing larger letters slows down
production speed. A larger letter would also take up more space on the writing sheet, and
originally the sheet was a scarce resource, while bulk, in the sense of larger or more sheets,
should be avoided. So, there are biomechanical and economic reasons for a maximum size
of letters. This raises the question whether letters could be even smaller. Again, there are
two reasons why they are not: (1) the physics of writing and (2) the perceiving of writing.

(1) physics of writing

First there are the specific properties of ink and paper. If letters are to be easily recognized they must have a high resolution. But paper has absorption and ink has flow properties. As a result, ink spills from the point of application outwards and so creates visual noise. It is clear that this noise should not obliterate the letter's contours, and therefore there is only one way to increase the S/N ratio: making letters much larger than the noise limit. This property for many centuries also held for print, as paper before 1900 had rather high absorption. Modern-day printing techniques can attain a very high resolution; ten lines/mm is attainable in all printing shops, which is about five times higher than the smallest detail of letters. Laser printers with 600 dpi can achieve 23 lines/mm, but their dots are less well defined than in conventional print.

(2) perceiving writing

The other reason for the size of writing is the resolution of our visual system. Looking at the transfer from print to vision - technically the contrast sensitivity function (see Farrell, 1991) - there is a clear optimum around 8 c/d[4]. This optimal region corresponds very closely to the fundamental spatial frequency of the individual letter positions and the more detailed structure within them. The shape of the function is such that the serifs - the cross-bars at the end of letters - are still well visible, while for even smaller details the function falls off very rapidly. Thus it appears that normal text, as we write and print it is optimally suited for our visual system. There is nothing that we can see better than text.

Print quality is still superior by far to the rendering quality of any current CRT or LCD screen. Many other features of print on paper also favour its use. Its physical character implies that it has a location, and people are quite good at remembering locations. Cicero recommended the memory for locations as an effective memorizing tool. We can remember where documents are: locations drive our search. But there is no such a stable structure for digital documents since they have no meaningful physical location. Also, real documents have physical characteristics, such as size and shape, that are not easily represented in digital form. In computers we have the desktop metaphor, but this is no more than a window on closed or opened documents. Each document is also a window, all of them neatly aligned, straightened up, without dog ears or creases, that make the comparison with one's own desk a humiliating experience. No digital document has coffee stains, there are nowhere scribbles, corrections or faint traces of lipstick. The digital document has its incontestable advantages, but it lacks also many useful features; some that are the essential 'reason for being' of documents.

---

4   c/d: c is to be conceived as a cycle of a one-dimensional sinusoidal modulation whereas d is the degree of the visual angle. One degree of visual angle subtends approximately 1 cm at normal reading distance.

5   Communication

The most important property of the document, however, is its communicative value. In essence, any document is a multicast, (or one point-to-many-points) communication with no feedback. The oldest form of flexible and productive communication is undoubtedly spoken language, especially in the form of a person to person dialogue. We know that a dialogue is a very powerful way of exchanging information, even if we are hardly aware of it, because of its commonness, its frequency and its ease. But it is also well known that in spoken communication many misunderstandings, breaks, corrections, repetitions and confirmations occur. In actual counts in real conversations, about 50% of all utterances are of this kind (Bunt, 1995). They are called dialogue control utterances and serve only to control the information flow, but do not contain elements of the information itself.
A schematic picture of the basic communication loop is shown in figure 3.

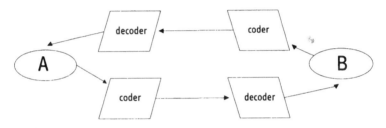

Figure 3.
Schematic diagram of the communication protocol between two partners A and B.
A is the originator, sending a message via its coder to B, which decodes it and responds similarly.

It is based on so-called reference models for communication in networks (Taylor, 1988a, 1988b). The idea is that the communicating partners, A and B, have the intention to transfer knowledge to the other partner. As thoughts cannot be transferred directly, the message has to be transformed into a form suitable for transmission, which is essentially what the 'coder' does. The content of the message has to be decoded by B, in order to make it part of the knowledge of B. In spoken communication, coding refers to a sequence of different processes, including selection, formulation, pronunciation and articulation, while decoding comprises hearing, identifying speech sounds, recognizing words, understanding sentences and extracting the gist of the message. If, after the perception of the message, a misunderstanding of whatever sort should arise, B can compile a counter-message in a coding process and send it on to A, who can decode, and understand it. Such a message by B may be a confirmation, but also a request for clarification. It is the existence of this loop, over which messages of various kinds referring to the content of the messages and the transmission of the messages are being exchanged that supports, or even determines successful communication. When there is feedback from the receiver B to A, this will signal to the originator A that his message has been received successfully, or has been understood. If this is not the case he can take appropriate action until there is evidence that the intended knowledge items are shared by both partners (Taylor, Néel & Bouwhuis, 1989).

In actual life, both participants in a conversation employ feedback extensively. How then does communication on the basis of a document succeed without direct feedback? The somewhat resigned answer has to be that, most of the time, it does not. Notorious examples are forms that are practically never filled in completely and correctly. Research by Jansen (1988) showed that in some cases 95% of all forms were completed incorrectly, resulting in wrong decisions being taken by the receiving agency. With simple changes, the error score could be reduced considerably, but there is preciously little evidence that current error scores are much below 20%. This phenomenon reveals one of the most important shortcomings of paper documents. Their permanence and stability, valued properties for some purposes, also imply a lack of interactivity, and so turn into distinct disadvantages for other purposes, mostly those related to understanding. The communication protocol in this case looks like that in figure 4, which is an incomplete version of that in figure 3. It is useful to note that a symmetry property has also been broken.

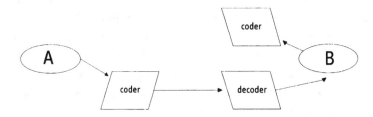

Figure 4.
The communication protocol in the case of a document originating from A, requesting information from B. The coder represents the document, behind which the originator is unreachable. B's coder can only supply information for the document; B cannot communicate with respect to its correctness or suitability.

Figure 4 depicts the situation from B's point of view. B observes a document (the result of A's coder); may or may not decode it successfully, but cannot ask A questions about it. Paper documents cannot respond to questions. At the same time A supposes that the communication loop is unbroken as soon as information, as a result of the request to B, arrives. But within the constraints of form filling, A has no way of ensuring that the information supplied is correct. The widespread use of fill-in forms is clearly motivated by economic reasons. It is by far the cheapest method of collecting information from large groups of people. Yet, it can only be successful when there is a high degree of standardization that the group of users of such documents knows and accepts.
Such documents presuppose knowledge of a specific kind, such that both successful decoding and correct coding are guaranteed. If both happen no feedback is necessary.

With the growing information needs in our society and the proliferation of different forms, such standardization has become all but impossible and, as a consequence, both understandability and certainty of communication suffer. While completed forms may look organized and systematic, there is no certainty that the information provided by the person who received the form is correct according to the criteria of the agency who sent it. Different ways have been devised to increase the accuracy of requested information. Forms can be made very redundant, sometimes asking for the same things in different contexts. Sometimes instructions are supplied. In other cases designers have reduced the information questions to forms that only require YES or NO answers. By answering a series of these interdependent questions organized in a tree form, the required information can be identified at the final stage. In many cases this could have also been dealt with by means of a single, but very complex question that certainly would have resulted in many wrong responses.

Nevertheless, it seems that current graphical tools and techniques from various fields predispose document designers to spend more effort on design than on communicative success. An interesting case in this respect is the Dutch tax form that was substantially modified in 1989 in the hope of a better understanding by the citizen. The authorities were quite pleased with the reform. It turned out that this was largely because of the reduction in the number of pages, resulting in a lower weight. The corresponding reduction in postage costs then paid back the investment in form redesign in an unexpectedly short time. However, whatever measures are taken to increase the reliability of form information, the lack of feedback in the case of paper forms means that reliability will always be sub-optimal. Reinstating feedback would cause long handling times, but, especially when more iterations would be necessary, would also be prohibitively expensive.

6   The digital document

Information technology has brought us the digital document, which does not even have a real material representation. The basic physical, but temporary representation is the visual one, mediated by the screen. To this may be added auditory information which, like the visual information, may be time-variant or dynamic. Despite the greater complexity that is attainable with the digital document, it is still easier to produce than its paper counterpart, because of the many tools that are available to the computer user. It is not always realized that the rise of the digital document, the production of which came within the reach of all computer users, often replaced long-standing typographical traditions. In fact, most people using the graphical tools are hardly aware of the existence of such traditions and so violate many typographical rules in blissful ignorance. In an attempt to emulate the printed document as closely as possible typographical conventions had to be adopted in text processors. This confronted users with an array of options, the functions of which escape many a naive user. Seen in the framework of the communication protocol, the user composing a message lacks knowledge on how to code it, to bring it into a shape suitable for transmission. As with most products, the user cannot ask the designer of the software program for explanation and assistance. The conventional solution is to provide a user manual. However, the complexity of software programs is such that manuals tend to become extremely detailed and voluminous, and mostly come in several parts: the thinner one of which is invariably called 'Getting started'. It is well known that manuals are only rarely consulted; actual studies of computer users show that most knowledge of commands and procedures is acquired by asking colleagues, irrespective of the availability and ease of manuals. This is not illogical; trying to find specific information in one or more books is more demanding than asking a colleague on the spot. In addition, this colleague may well have experience with the problem and add valuable information, such as shortcuts or actions to be avoided. In fact, the documentation that came with a computer became so bulky and expensive to produce that it was the first information to be recorded entirely on the new CD-ROM medium, a course that was pioneered by DEC. This made it not only possible, but almost essential to have on-screen help functions that read the corresponding information from the CD-ROM and so obviated the need for printed books. Especially in the early phases it was not always easy to obtain information about all conceivable functions, but at least all the information about the computer system and its functions was combined in a single package. Search through books was replaced by typing simple requests for help. The increase in power of personal computers and the corresponding extension of functionality also pushed developments in a similar direction, so that not only operating systems, but many application packages are now released on a CD-ROM with the help functions integrated. Thus, for most software applications, and certainly text processors, on-screen help is the norm and has been considerably expanded from its humble beginnings.

On-screen help has a number of additional advantages over books; being integrated with the software application it can be made context dependent. On the Apple Macintosh, for example, 'help' on functions is provided in the form of a dialogue in which the user is asked to carry out an action, see the result and then gets the next instruction, until the whole function has been explained. This procedure mimics a teacher-student interaction, where there is a continuous sequence of teacher instructions and student actions. Coupling the instruction so directly to the action precludes the student from taking other actions than those instructed. This dependency cannot be achieved by the use of a book, where the user is free to carry out or not to carry out the actions correctly. A book has no feedback.

The on-screen help effectively provides the direct feedback that is missing in books, and so closes the communication loop. (see figure 5). However, now the communication loop is a modest one, that of the user communicating with a system in order to make a document.

It is only one step towards the communication between two human partners, A and B, which comprises a much larger loop. Basically, on-screen help functions enable A to clarify the purpose of his communication to B by means of a document that provides optimal opportunities for knowledge transfer.

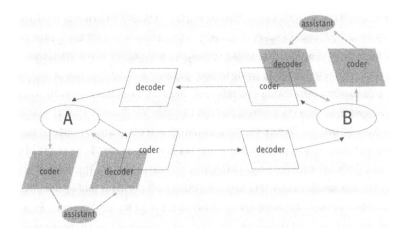

Figure 5.
The communication protocol in which 'assistants' have been added that are implemented as help functions in composing the document to be forwarded. For some functions, the decoder of the help function carries out parts of the coding directly. Note that both partners have a help function, which is different for a fill-in form.

It should be clear that the ultimate success of this endeavour can only be judged when A has obtained information from B that can be trusted to be valid. This is not always easy to decide, as the communication loop, shown in figure 5 is getting even more complex. Just as A may need help to compose or optimize his document, B may need help to answer the questions, or to give the information requested in A's document. Therefore, on-line instruction may be available to B, which, logically takes the same form as that for A, and expands the communication loop at its side. There is no doubt that the availability of these interactive help-functions may be particularly helpful, both for the originator and the sender.

However, at the same time it is clear that the total number of interfaces, represented by coders and decoders, is increasing. Each interface introduces its own uncertainties in communication. Developers of help functions, assistants and various other forms of on-screen help often seem to think that only the task is in need of assistance, but not the assistant itself. Of course, this is a self-defeating argument: if the user has trouble in executing a task, this must be due in large part to the interface, but since the assistant must also have an interface, it will necessitate another assistant and so on. A number of computer operating systems indeed have something like 'help help', where the second argument is the actual help function. So far a function like 'help help help' seems to lead to the notification of a syntax error. In this sense it is a favourable property that the interfaces are more parallel than serial in structure. What this comes down to is that a user, who cannot make any sense of the help-function can nevertheless still create a message which, while graphically and grammatically unacceptable, may still do the job.

Before one jumps to the conclusion that it is only the content of the message that matters, it has to be borne in mind that all messages have both content and form. Form is empty, but content has to have a carrier which, by definition, has to have form. But form has to have a physical representation for it to be perceived effectively by a human being. As mentioned earlier, this representation needs not to be one on paper, it may be visual or auditory, but it will always have to be rendered within the constraints of human perception. This is not the place to give a detailed description of the hierarchical properties of the perceptual system, except that this system makes use of a large number of organizing principles that must be matched in the appearance of a stimulus pattern such as a document. Not all of these principles are 'hard-wired' - built into our nervous system - but many of them are learnt during prolonged exposure and have shaped our processes of decoding and comprehension. Reading text is an example of this, which includes processes to distinguish black and white edges on a white surface, up to reasoning processes concerned with memorized events. Creating text involves a number of steps. Letters need to be created, or an existing type face selected. These letters are used to put words together following the rules of spelling. Next, words have to be strung into lines and paragraphs, where they have to make sentences following the rules of syntax and grammar. A clear and attractive writing style has to be adopted for the targeted audience. All of these steps have the objective of achieving the best possible transfer of message content. It is frequently underestimated to what extent the lower layers of the rendering concerned with form affect the efficiency with which the content can be understood. It is exactly for that reason that typography is important, and it is for that reason that typesetting programs are based on typographical tradition. The way print looks nowadays, helps us to read it. That many typographers do not know in what way typography affects human perceptual processes is immaterial, it is more our human experience with print that counts than the exact details that are used in rendering it.

In this respect it is interesting to note that practically no text processing program provides directed means to make a table that conforms to international standardization rules. Neither WordPerfect, *Latex*, nor Word in its many versions help the user in drawing up a table as it should look according to international standards. Surprisingly, styles for tables are published in all style sheets and publication manuals of scientific journals, but are apparently completely overlooked in developing text processors. One of the most elementary errors is that the user is completely free to put the table caption under the table, whereas all standardization bodies prescribe that it should appear above the table. This could be very easily implemented, but is not done systematically. Actually, most standardization rules go even further in stipulating that the first word of the caption should be the noun phrase (noun plus modifiers) describing the items in the body of the table. In order to be really helpful, such information on rules could be easily supplied by the assistant when creating a table environment, but this has apparently never been implemented by the developers.

Line spacing, or 'leading', is another example. If consecutive lines are too closely packed, the eye, having arrived at the end of one line, has difficulty finding the beginning of the next line, and may easily skip one. It has been established empirically that the length of lines should not exceed 20 times the line spacing, and preferably be somewhat shorter. This can be theoretically understood by taking into account the interference between the first characters of two lines as a function of the distance between them, and the distance they are removed from the point of fixation. From the end of one line, the eye has to aim at the beginning of the next line on the basis of what is visible of the left-hand side of the text. If the angle of the return sweep is too small, the available visual information may not be sufficient to guide the eye to the correct new location. In a digital document, there are no longer the same constraints that hold for line spacing in the printing environment. Lines can be as closely packed and as long as desired, and there is nowhere any warning that this will seriously reduce readability catastrophically. The Internet shows many examples of well-intended detailed information that is impossible to read because of close line spacing and long lines. The balance between information value and communicative value seems to shift often in the direction of information value, at the expense of communicative value. It needs no further explanation that if the latter is affected the first is becoming useless.

Lest this discussion may seem to concentrate on boring, and purely formal details, it should be pointed out that the function of a table is to aid the communication. By standardizing the organization of tables, so that things mean invariably the same, the perceptual and cognitive system of the reader is considerably supported in decoding and understanding. Few people would dispute that language has a spelling, and that words should be spelt according to that spelling. In fact, spell checkers are some of the most valued parts of text processors. While original minds may balk at the idea, spelling is one of the most basic standardization's that we have, which not only eases reading, but makes it possible. Without spelling there would never have been reading. This is not to say that spelling is ideal (in principle in the alphabetic system it cannot be), or that we cannot live with an incidental typo, but we cannot do without its organizing principle. A similar thing holds for tables. As soon as one grasps the basic concepts behind the organizing principle of a table, its contents become clear at once and its structure seems inescapable.

7   Form, appearance and attention

Form has many aspects. Form can be shaped in ways limited only by imagination. One of
the prerequisites of communication is to draw the receiver into the communicative loop. In
a document this cannot be achieved by turn-taking, as in speech, so the attention of the
other has to be gained. It is not surprising that text processors and typesetting programs are
brimming with just such features in order to draw attention. Also then the question remains
whether, if attention has been gained, the document itself serves its communicative
purpose. It is astonishing to observe how often document designers prefer form over
content. Graphical features fancied by a designer will generally prevail over requirements
for optimal perception and understanding. One example, becoming ever more frequent, is
printing text over a picture background, something that can be very easily realized with
current graphical software packages. Conceptual, picture and text are wholly different. If the
picture has to gain attention, it is the text that becomes the background. If the text is the
focus of attention, the picture is the background. Both cannot be foreground at the same
time, even if they have been explicitly designed as the proverbial integrated whole. Picture
and text will necessarily interfere with each other in the visual system, however enticing the
picture; however compelling the text, and however striking the combination. No property of
text or printing technique can undo this interference, and both picture and text will suffer as
a consequence. But the main question remains whether ultimately understanding has
benefited from the advances in graphical design.

8   The technological context

In the development of digital typography, the tools for creating text and its layout were so
different from those of conventional printing that its course was largely dissociated from
established printing tradition. It is hardly surprising that many of the traditions from the
printing trade were violated in ignorance, and in full awareness of the arrival of a better
world in printing. But print is not an island. Print plays its part in the interaction of a reader
with text, and cannot be seen as developing on its technical merits only. Print lives by virtue
of a human reader, imbued with a visual system, with knowledge and experience. The
available computing power to generate new graphical styles, and the speed at which this
could be realized has fooled many digital designers into the belief that superior methods for
the generation of text and graphics have finally become available. There is no doubt that
these methods are superior, and will even get better still. And though the looks of the
document may be impressive, the real question is whether this makes the document better
readable and comprehensible. Even cursory studies on performance of reading from
computer screens shows that this is impressively not the case.

9   Navigation and the spatial environment

Digital documents have the obvious advantages of easy and economic storage and fast and
accurate retrieval. Essentially, there is no such thing as somewhere in a computer memory,
not even in the physical sense. Files are stored somewhere on a physical medium, but are
almost always fragmented, where the individual components refer to each other's location
by means of pointers that are invisible at the user level. As noted before, this is very
different from existing physical objects. Objects, and also documents, must be somewhere,
in a single place, and at a location that can be specified by reference to other locations in
the space surrounding the user. So, in a physical environment the user has considerably
more cues to retrieve a document than in the virtual world of digital documents. It would be
highly recommendable that a storage environment for digital documents would be
designed, in which users could retrieve documents in an effective and acceptable way.

However, this is only half of the story. A paper document is in the hands of the reader,
literally and metaphorically. The reader controls the process of scanning by means of eye
movements, focusing and shifting attention, moving the page up, or down, or moving to
following or previous pages. The permanent nature of the paper document implies that this
human control is a form of 'total' control[5]. This again, is very different with digital
documents. As a rule only part of the document is shown on the screen. In the virtual world
all is there, but will require manual scrolling. The scrolling process is dissimilar to a
scanning process, as it cannot be guided by comprehensive visual inspection. Every
scrolling action is an act of reconnaissance, in which the reader discovers the existence of
material that was invisible before. Beyond a single 'page', things get progressively worse.
When the document consists of many pages, structured in a linear or hierarchical way
wayfinding becomes much more difficult and proper navigational aids have to be given in
order to ease the human search process. Though hypertext has been proposed as an
efficient way to navigate through structured material, empirical studies have demonstrated
that only designers benefit from hypertext navigation, and then only when they traverse
their own application. Casual, and especially elderly users have difficulties in navigation
that seem aggravated by hypertext rather than taken away. Complex forms nowadays
already cope with navigation problems, when users have to fill in information specific to
their own situation. When the design of such forms is seen as a challenge, then the digital
fill-in form has a lot more in store.

---

5   Assuming that the user is not motorically handicapped.

10 Interaction

The real difference that a digital document can make is interactivity. Depending on the navigational actions and the responses of the reader to requests in the document, feedback can be given. Feedback is the principal means by which communication can be established, a feature that is absent in passive documents. It is not the case that feedback is a panacea; setting up a protocol for a smooth and continuous dialogue is not a trivial issue. But feedback could overcome one of the inherent drawbacks of paper documents to the extent that they cannot ensure understanding, and, inasmuch it has been evaluated experimentally, rarely do so effectively. Improvements on this aspect will mostly be of a marginal nature, irrespective of the inherent value of the paper document. Perhaps the digital document will never replace the paper document for reasons of reliability, permanence, trust and readability. But the digital document has other valuable properties. Yet, it is clear that this value can only be realized if the properties and the behaviour of the digital document can be closely matched to human behaviour.

References

- Bouwhuis, D.G. (1989), *Reading as goal-driven behaviour.* In: B.A.G. Elsendoorn and H. Bouma (eds.), Working models of human perception. London, Academic Press, p. 341-362.
- Bouwhuis, D.G. (1993), *Reading rate and letter size.* Eindhoven, IPO Annual Progress Report 28, p. 30-36.
- Bunt, H.C. (1995), *Dialogue control functions and interaction design.* In: R.J. Beun, M. Reiner and M. Baker, (eds.), *Dialogue and instruction, modeling interaction in intelligent tutoring systems.* NATO ASI Series, F 142. Berlin, Springer p. 197-214.
- Coe, M.D. (1992), *Breaking the Maya Code.* London, Thames & Hudson.
- Farrell, J.E. (1991), *Fitting physical screen parameters to the human eye.* In: J.R. Cronly-Dillon (ed.), Vision and visual dysfunction, Vol. 15: The man-machine interface, J.A.J. Roufs (ed.). Basingstoke, Macmillan Press, p. 7-23.
- Gelb, I. (1952), *A study of writing.* Chicago, University of Chicago Press.
- Gordon, C.H. (1962), *Before the Bible: The common background of Greek and Hebrew civilizations.* New York, Harper & Row.
- Powell, M.A. (1982), *Three problems in the history of cuneiform writing: origins, direction of script, literacy.* Visible Language, XV, p. 419-440.
- Schmandt-Besserat, D. (1981), *From tokens to tablets: A re-evaluation of the so-called 'numerical tablets'.* Visible Language XV, p. 321-344.
- Taylor, M.M. (1988a), *Layered protocols for computer-human dialogue. I: Principles.* International journal of man-machine studies 28, p. 175-218.
- Taylor, M.M. (1988a), *Layered protocols for computer-human dialogue. II: Some practical issues.* International journal of man-machine studies. 28, p. 219-257.
- Taylor, M.M., Néel, F. and Bouwhuis, D.G. (eds.) (1989), *The structure of multimodal dialogue.* Amsterdam, North-Holland.
- Tombaugh, J., Lickorish, A. and Wright, P. (1987), *Multi-window displays for readers of lengthy text.* International journal of man-machine studies 26, p. 597-615.
- Valladas, H., Reyss, J.L., Joron, J.L., Valladas, G., Bar-Yosef, O. and Vandermeersch, B. (1988), *Thermoluminescence dating of Mousterian 'Proto-Crô-Magnon' remains from Israel and the origin of modern man.* Nature 331, p. 614-616.

About the author

Dominic Bouwhuis studied psychology at Nijmegen University in The Netherlands and published his dissertation Visual recognition of words in 1979. Since 1968 he has been attached to the Institute for Perception Research (IPO), Eindhoven. Since 1987 he has been an evaluator of various IT framework projects of the European Community. Since 1988 he is professor of technical psychonomics at the Eindhoven University of Technology. His interests center on interactive instruction and human-computer communication. In 1991 he started research on cognition and aging, especially in relation to the use of technology by elderly users.